# GRANNY'S MELTING POT

## Mae T. Adams

Copyright © 1997 / 2014 by Mae T. Adams
All rights reserved.
Published 2014

Published by VIP Ink Publishing, L.L.C.
www.vipinkpublishing.com

For information about special discounts for bulk purchases, please contact VIP Ink Publishing, L.L.C. special sales department at business@vipinkpublishing.com

Cover Design and Book Layout by Sarah McClain.
www.thewritesarah.com

All rights reserved.

No part of this book may be reproduced, stored in a retrieval system, or transmitted, in any form or by any means, electronic or mechanical, including photocopying and recording without prior written permission from the publisher.

Adams, Mae T.
Granny's Melting Pot
First Edition Print

ISBN 13: 978-1-939670-07-6
ISBN: 978-1-939670-07-6
Printed in the USA.

# Measurements Conversion Chart

## US DRY VOLUME MEASUREMENTS

| Measure | Equivalent |
|---|---|
| 1/16 teaspoon | dash |
| 1/8 teaspoon | a pinch |
| 3 teaspoons | 1 Tablespoon |
| 1/8 cup | 2 tablespoons (=1 standard coffee scoop) |
| 1/4 cup | 4 Tablespoons |
| 1/3 cup | 5 Tablespoons plus 1 teaspoon |
| 1/2 cup | 8 Tablespoons |
| 3/4 cup | 12 Tablespoons |
| 1 cup | 16 Tablespoons |
| 1 Pound | 16 ounces |

## US LIQUID VOLUME MEASUREMENTS

| | |
|---|---|
| 8 Fluid ounces | 1 Cup |
| 1 Pint | 2 Cups (= 16 fluid ounces) |
| 1 Quart | 2 Pints (= 4 cups) |
| 1 Gallon | 4 Quarts (= 16 cups) |

## US TO METRIC CONVERSIONS

| | |
|---|---|
| 1/5 teaspoon | 1 ml (=milliliter, one thousandth of a liter) |
| 1 teaspoon | 5 ml |
| 1 tablespoon | 15 ml |
| 1 fluid oz. | 30 ml |
| 1/5 cup | 50 ml |
| 1 cup | 240 ml |
| 2 cups (1 pint) | 470 ml |
| 4 cups (1 quart) | .95 liter |
| 4 quarts (1 gal.) | 3.8 liters |
| 1 oz. | 28 grams |
| 1 pound | 454 grams |

## METRIC TO US CONVERSIONS

| Metric | US |
|---|---|
| 1 milliliter | 1/5 teaspoon |
| 5 ml | 1 teaspoon |
| 15 ml | 1 tablespoon |
| 30 ml | 1 fluid oz. |
| 100 ml | 3.4 fluid oz. |
| 240 ml | 1 cup |
| 1 liter | 34 fluid oz. |
| 1 liter | 4.2 cups |
| 1 liter | 2.1 pints |
| 1 liter | 1.06 quarts |
| 1 liter | .26 gallon |
| 1 gram | .035 ounce |
| 100 grams | 3.5 ounces |
| 500 grams | 1.10 pounds |
| 1 kilogram | 2.205 pounds |
| 1 kilogram | 35 oz. |

## PAN SIZE EQUIVALENTS

| | |
|---|---|
| 9-by-13-in. baking dish | 22-by-33-cm (centimeter) baking dish |
| 8-by-8-in. baking dish | 20-by-20-cm baking dish |
| 9-by-5-in. loaf pan | 23-by-12-cm loaf pan (=8 c. or 2 liters) |
| 10-in. tart or cake pan | 25-cm tart or cake pan |
| 9-in. cake pan | 22-cm cake pan |

## OVEN TEMPERATURE CONVERSIONS

| Fahrenheit | Celsius | Gas Mark |
|---|---|---|
| 275° F | 140° C | gas mark 1-cool |
| 300° F | 150° C | gas mark 2 |
| 325° F | 165° C | gas mark 3-very moderate |
| 350° F | 180° C | gas mark 4-moderate |
| 375° F | 190° C | gas mark 5 |
| 400° F | 200° C | gas mark 6-moderately hot |
| 425° F | 220° C | gas mark 7- hot |
| 450° F | 230° C | gas mark 9 |
| 475° F | 240° C | gas mark 10- very hot |

## RATIOS FOR SELECTED FOODS

**MEASURE** . . . . . . . . . . . . . . **EQUIVALENT**

**Butter**

| | | | |
|---|---|---|---|
| 1 T. | 14 grams | 1 T. | |
| 1 stick | 4 ou=113 grams | 8 T. | ½ cup |
| 4 sticks | 16 ou=452 grams | 32 tablespoons | 2 cups |

**Lemon**

| | | |
|---|---|---|
| 1 lemon | 1 to 3 T. juice, | 1 to 1½ tsp grated zest |
| 4 large lemons | 1 cup juice | ¼ cup grated zest |

**Chocolate**

| | |
|---|---|
| 1 ounce | ¼ cup grated 40 grams |
| 6 ounces chips | 1 cup chips 160 grams |
| cocoa powder | 1 cup 115 grams |

**Creams**

| | | |
|---|---|---|
| Half and half | ½ milk ½ cream | 10.5-18 % butterfat |
| Light cream | | 18% butterfat |
| Light whipping cream | | 26-30% butterfat |
| Heavy cream | whipping cream | 36% or more butterfat |
| Double cream | extra-thick double cream, Clotted or Devonshire | 42 % butterfat |

## MEASURES FOR PANS AND DISHES

**INCHES** . . . . . . . . . . . . . . . . **CENTIMETERS**

| | |
|---|---|
| 9-by-13-in. baking dish | 22-by-33-cm (centimeter) baking dish |
| 8-by-8-in. baking dish | 20-by-20-cm baking dish |
| 9-by-5-in. loaf pan (8 c.) | 23-by-12-cm loaf pan (2 liters) |
| 10-in. tart or cake pan | 25-cm tart or cake pan |
| 9-in. cake pan | 22-cm cake pan |

# "HEAVEN'S GROCERY STORE"

I was walking down life's highway a long time ago.
One day I saw a sign that read,

"HEAVEN'S GROCERY STORE"

As I got a little closer
the door came open wide
And when I came to myself
I was standing inside.

I saw a host of **ANGELS**.
They were standing everywhere.
One handed me a basket and said,
"My Child shop with care".

Everything a Christian needed
was in that grocery store.
And all you couldn't carry,
you could come back the next day for more.

First, I got some **PATIENCE**:
**LOVE** was in the same row.
Further down was **UNDERSTANDING**:
You need that everywhere you go.

I got a box or two of **WISDOM**,
a bag or two of **FAITH**.
I just couldn't miss the **HOLY GHOST**,
For it was all over the place.

I stopped to get some **STRENGTH** and **COURAGE**
To help me run this race.
By then my basket was getting full,
But I remembered I needed some **GRACE**.

I didn't forget **SALVATION**,
For **SALVATION** was free,
So I tried to get enough of that
To save both You and Me.

Then I started up to the counter
To pay my grocery bill,
For I thought I had everything
To do the **MASTER'S** Will.

As I went up the aisle, I saw **PRAYER**:
And I just had to put that in,
For I knew when I stepped outside,
I would run into Sin.

**PEACE AND JOY** were plenty
They were last on the shelf.
**SONG** and **PRAISE** were hanging near,
So I just helped myself.

Then I said to the angel,
"Now, how much do I owe?"
He smiled and said,
"Just take them everywhere you go."

Again, I smiled and said,
"How much do I really owe?"
He smiled again and said,
***"MY CHILD, JESUS PAID YOUR BILL
A LONG, LONG TIME AGO."***

Author Unknown

# Artichoke Balls

**Ingredients:**
3 Cloves Garlic, Chopped Fine
1 Small Onion, Chopped Fine
2 - 14 oz Cans Artichoke Heart
1 ½ tsp Dry Parsley Flakes
1 Cup Seasoned Bread Crumbs
2 Tbsp Olive Oil
2 Tbsp Lemon Juice
2 Eggs, Beaten
Parmesan Cheese
¼ tsp Salt

**Directions:**
1. Preheat oven to 325° F.
2. Drain artichoke hearts, squeezing out extra juice and blend until smooth, set aside.
3. In a pan sauté onion and garlic in the olive oil. Mix in artichoke and eggs. Cook until eggs are no longer runny (about 5 minutes). Remove from heat, set aside.
4. In medium mixing bowl, add bread crumbs, lemon juice, salt, and parsley flakes. Stir in the artichokes and mix well. Chill until set (about 4 hours).
5. Grease a sheet pan and form chilled artichoke mix into balls. Roll artichoke balls into cheese and place on sheet pan. Bake for 25 - 30 minutes.

# Apple Butter

**Ingredients:**
6 Large Cooking Apples (Rome or Winesap)
1 tsp Cinnamon, Ground
1 tsp Cloves, Ground
3 Cups Apple Cider
½ tsp Allspice
2 Cups Water
2 ½ Cups Sugar

**Directions:**
1. Wash, core and slice apples. Place sliced apples in large pot with water and cook until soft (about 10 minutes).
2. Force soft apples through a sieve to remove the peels, set aside.
3. In large pot heat apple cider to boiling.
4. Add half as much sugar as you have mashed apples (usually around 2½ cups) and stir until sugar is dissolved.
5. Reduce heat and add mashed apples, cinnamon, clove and allspice.
6. Stir frequently to prevent the mix from sticking to pan and until the apple butter is thick enough to spread.
7. Spoon into glass jars tighten lids and place in a hot water bath for 10 minutes or store in the refrigerator.

# Cajun Pepper Jelly

**Ingredients:**
1 Cup Water or Apple Juice
½ Bottle Fruit Pectin
½ tsp Tabasco Sauce
3 Drops Food Coloring, Green***
3 Cups Sugar
⅓ Cup Green Peppers Chopped***

**Directions:**
1. In a heavy pot combine sugar, water (or apple juice), peppers and Tabasco sauce. Heat until boiling, about 10 minutes.
2. Add food coloring and pectin; reduce heat to medium and let cook until it returns to boiling, about 5 minutes. It should "sheet", meaning when a spoon is placed in the mixture it is held up.
3. Pour mixture into 4 STERILIZED ½ pint jelly jars.
4. Serve over cream cheese with crackers.

******Red peppers and food coloring may used in place of the green, it is all a matter choice, hot or mild.

# Creole Seasoning Mix

**Ingredients:**
1 ½ Tbsp Onion Powder^
1 ½ Tbsp Garlic Powder*
¼ Salt
Tbsp Ground Red Pepper
2 Tbsp Black or White Pepper, Ground

**Directions:**
1. Mix all ingredients together well.
2. Place in a covered jar or salt shaker
3. Use like salt

* Garlic Powder, not Garlic Salt     ^Onion Powder, not Onion Salt

# Egg Rolls

### Ingredients:
1 Can Bamboo Shoots, Cut
Egg Roll Wraps
2 Stems Celery, Slice Thin
1 Cup Water Chestnuts, Cut
1 lb Ground Beef or Pork
1 Bag Cabbage, Slaw Mix
½ lb Bean Sprouts
1 Onion, Minced Fine
1 Bottle Soy Sauce
½ lb Small Shrimp (Peeled & De-veined)

### Directions:
1. Brown ground beef in pan, set aside.
2. Chop shrimp into small pieces.
3. Mix ground beef, shrimp, bamboo, celery, bean sprouts, water chestnuts, cabbage and onion in large pot. I use an electric wok.
4. Add soy sauce and cook until shrimp is pink and cabbage is wilted.
5. Remove from heat and let cool.
6. Spoon the mix into the egg roll wrappers and deep fry.

*Makes 70–90 egg rolls*

# Homemade Noodles

**Ingredients:**
5 Cups Flour
4 Eggs, Lightly Beaten
2/3 Cups Ice Water
Hot Soup, Stew or Broth

**Directions:**
1. Combine flour and eggs into a mixing bowl.
2. Add water. *You may need to use more or less than what is listed here. I have found humidity plays a part in the amount of water needed.*
3. Use your hands to work mixture into a stiff dough and knead until bubbles begin to form under the surface.
4. On a lightly floured table roll out dough to about ⅛ of an inch thick. The thinner you can roll it the better.
5. Sprinkle a little flour over the rolled dough and let the dough rest for about 20 minutes to dry.
6. Cut the dough into noodle strips
7. Drop handfuls of the noodles into any boiling liquid (soup, stew, broth etc.).
8. Cook 15 - 20 minutes, stirring often to prevent noodles from sticking.

*Makes 6–8 servings*

## Hot Crab and Cheese Dip

**Ingredients:**
8 oz. Cream Cheese
1 Stick Butter
1 lb Crab Meat
1 Onion, Minced
⅛ tsp Hot Sauce
⅛ tsp Garlic Powder
⅛ tsp Cayenne Pepper

**Directions:**
1. Over low heat melt butter and slowly stir in cream cheese.
2. Add crab meat and stir well.
3. Add onion, garlic powder, cayenne pepper and hot sauce; stir well.
4. Continue to cook until the cheese is just melted and the crab meat is heated through, about 5 minutes.
5. Serve with crackers or chips.

*Yields about 3 cups*

## Hot Crab Meat Dip

**Ingredients:**
1 ½ tsp Worcestershire Sauce
1 Tbsp Onions, Chopped
2 Pinches Black Pepper
1 lb Crab Meat
1 Egg, Slightly Beaten
2 Tbsp Flour
2 Tbsp Butter, Melted
1 ½ Cup Milk
¼ tsp Garlic Powder
½ tsp Salt

**Directions:**
1. In a bowl blend the flour, salt, pepper and garlic powder.
2. Pout melted butter in pan and add onions. Cook on medium heat for about five minutes.
3. Stir the flour mix into the pan with the butter and onions.
4. Add the milk slowly and stir slowly and constantly. Cook until thick.
5. Reduce heat to very low and add egg, stir well and stir often for about five minutes.
6. Add crab meat and simmer for 12 to 15 minutes.
7. Serve hot with crackers.

*Makes 2 cups*

## Hush Puppies

**Ingredients:**
2 Cups Yellow Corn Meal
1 Cup Onion, Minced Very Fine
1 Tbsp Baking Powder
1 Cup Flour
2 tsp Sugar
2 tsp Salt
2 Eggs Milk

**Directions:**
1. In a mixing bowl stir ingredients together.
2. Use just enough milk to moisten the dough to a stiff consistency, but not soft enough to spoon.
3. Dip with a tablespoon and drop into deep fryer (350°)
4. Cook until golden brown.
5. Serve with fried fish, fried crab, fried crayfish or fried shrimp and oysters.

*Makes 30 to 36*

# Oyster Stuffing

**Ingredients:**
3 dozen Oysters
4 Tbsp Fresh Parsley, Chopped
3 Large Onions, Chopped Fine
2 Cloves Garlic, Chopped Fine
3 Stalks Celery, Chopped Fine
½ Loaf French Bread, Stale
6 Green Onions, Chopped Fine
2 Large Eggs, Well Beaten
1 Tbsp Thyme
1 Stick Butter (or Oleo)
1 tsp Creole Seasoning (pg 3)
1 Green Bell Pepper, Chopped Fine

**Directions:**
1. Cut stale French bread into slices and place in water until soft. Squeeze the water from the bread and set aside.
2. Drain oysters, reserve liquid. Pick over oysters to be sure there are no shells and chop them.
3. Melt butter (or oleo) in a heavy pot.
4. Fry oysters and onions until tender (about 5 minutes)
5. Add celery, green onions, green bell pepper, parsley and garlic to the pot and cook for another 10 minutes.
6. Add the French bread, eggs and oysters to the pot. Let cook for five minutes, stir frequently.
7. Add the reserved oyster liquid, Creole seasoning, thyme, parsley and garlic to the pot and cook for another five minutes.
8. Use to stuff poultry or place in a casserole dish and bake at 350° F until done.

## Shrimp Dip

**Ingredients:**
2 Cloves Garlic, Chopped
1 lb Shrimp, Peeled & Divined
2 Tbsp Onions, Chopped
¼ tsp Black Pepper
1 Tbsp Worcestershire Sauce
1 Tbsp Hot Sauce
2 Tbsp Lemon Juice
1 tsp Salt
8 oz. Cream Cheese
Paprika

**Directions:**
1. Cook and drain shrimp. Set aside to cool.
2. Place cooled shrimp, garlic, onions, Worcestershire sauce, lemon juice, cream cheese, black pepper, hot sauce and salt in blender.
3. Cover and blend 1 minute or until smooth.
4. Pour into serving dish and chill 4 hours.
5. Sprinkle with paprika and serve with crackers.

*Yields 3 Cups*

# Tomato Marmalade

### Ingredients:
3 qt Ripe Tomacloves
2–4 Cinnamon Sticks, Broken
2 Tbsp Cloves, Whole
8–10 Cups Sugar
2 Lemons
2 Oranges

**Directions:**
1. Scald, drain and peel tomacloves, then cut into small pieces (there should be about 12 cups cut tomacloves).
2. Slice the lemons and oranges into very thin slices.
3. Pour off the juice from the tomacloves and add sugar. Stir until sugar is dissolved.
4. Add lemon and orange slices.
5. Tie the cinnamon and cloves into a loose cheese cloth bag and add to pot. Cook on high heat boiling rapidly until thick and clear.
6. Remove spice bag and pour tomacloves into sterilized glass jars. Leave about ¼' head space
7. Wipe each jar to remove any food that may have stuck.
8. Adjust caps and process for 20 minutes in a boiling hot water bath.

*Yields about 6 pints.*

# Tomato Roses

**Ingredients:**
4 Medium Tomacloves
8 oz Cream Cheese
2–3 Tbsp Milk
Red Food Coloring
1 Tbsp Mayonnaise
Paprika

**Directions:**
1. With electric mixer combine cream cheese, milk and enough red food coloring to make the mix a pretty pink color.
2. With a teaspoon, place spoonfuls of cream cheese mix in a row around the top of the tomato. This will look like a row of petals.
3. Now place a second row of cream cheese "petals" centering them between 2 petals of the first row.
4. Add a teaspoon of mayonnaise to the center of each tomato.
5. Sprinkle paprika on top of the mayonnaise.
6. Chill 3 to 4 hours

*Serve on a bed of leafy lettuce.*
*Serves 4*

# Roux

**Ingredients:**
½ Cup Oil
½ Cup Flour

**Directions:**
1. In pan heat oil on low heat
2. After the oil is warm slowly add flour while constantly stirring the mix with a whisk.
3. Watch roux carefully as it can burn quickly.

This is used as a base for many of the soups and gumbos in this section. Sometimes there may be different measures of oil and flour listed, but the method will not change. Follow the measures given in the individual recipes if they are different.

# Black-Eyed Pea Soup

**Ingredients:**
3 Cans Black Eyed Peas
¼ Cup Green Onions, Chopped
2 Cloves Garlic, Chopped
1 Medium Onion Chopped
¼ Cup Parsley Chopped
¼ Cup Celery Chopped
4 Tbsp Butter or Oleo
1 Bell Pepper Chopped
¾ lb Smoked Country Sausage or Ham
1 tsp Sweet Basil Flakes, Crushed
2 Cans Tomacloves, Stewed, Sliced, Seasoned

**Directions:**
1. Melt butter (or oleo) in a 4 qt sauce pan, add onions, celery, bell pepper, garlic, and green bell pepper. Cook until vegetables are limp, about five minutes.
2. Add the sausage, parsley and sweet basil. Cook for another five minutes.
3. Add the cans of black-eyed peas and the cans of tomacloves. Stir well.
4. Add enough water to rinse out the cans and make a soup.
5. Cook for 20 - 30 minutes.
6. Cook rice and set aside. DO NOT ADD TO SOUP!

Allow each person to serve themselves the amount
of rice and soup they desire.

*Serves 6 to 8*

# Chicken and Okra Gumbo

**Ingredients:**
2 Tbsp Creole Seasoning
2 Cubes Chicken Bouillon
1 Large Onion, Chopped
1 Bell Pepper, Chopped
6 Green Onions, Chopped
½ Cup Oil
3 Cloves Garlic, Chopped
½ Cup Flour
2 Cups Fresh Okra, Sliced
1 Chicken
1 Can Stewed Tomacloves
2 qt Water
¼ Cup Dry Parsley Flakes

**Directions:**
1. Cut up chicken, I always remove the skin and as much fat as possible.
2. Make a roux.
3. Add onions, green onions, parsley, bell pepper and garlic; Stir.
4. Add the chicken and brown a little before adding the water.
5. Add bouillon cubes to hot water and after dissolved add water to the roux. Cook on low heat for 40 minutes.
6. While chicken is cooking, in a heavy skillet heat the oil and add okra; stir frequently until all the slime is cooked out. (Do not use an iron pot/pan for this as it will turn the okra black!)
7. Add cooked okra and stewed tomacloves to gumbo.
8. Season to taste with Creole seasoning and salt.

*Serve over hot rice.*
*Makes 8 Servings*

## Chicken and Sausage Gumbo

**Ingredients:**
1 - 3lb Chicken, Skinned & Cut
1 Large Onion, Chopped
1 Clove Garlic, Chopped
2 Cubes Chicken Bouillon
¼ Cup Dry Parsley Flakes
¼ Cup Dry Green Pepper
6 Green Onions, Chopped
¼ Cup Flour
¼ Cup Oil
1 lb Smoked Sausage
Creole Seasoning to Taste
Salt & Pepper to Taste

**Directions:**
1. In a large pot mix cut chicken, onion, garlic, green onions, green peppers, and bouillon cubes. Cover with 4 quarts of water.
2. Cook for 1 hour or until tender. Remove from heat and let stand 30 minutes.
3. Take the chicken out of the water and pick me off of the bound, then place the chicken back into the pot.
4. Make a roux.
5. Add the roux to the chicken and cook for 15 minutes to thicken.
6. Add the sausage to the pot.
7. Add salt, pepper and Creole seasoning to taste.
8. Cook about 1 hour on very low heat, let cool.

*Serve hot over rice*
*Serves 6 to 8*

# Chili Con Con

**Ingredients:**
2 lb Lean Ground Beef
2 Large onions, Chopped
4 Tbsp Garlic Powder
2 - 6 oz Cans Tomato Paste
4 Cans Creamed Red Beans
Chili Powder to Taste
4 Cloves Garlic, Chopped
Water
2 Cans Seasoned Stewed Tomacloves, Sliced

**Directions:**
1. Cook the ground beef and drain all the fat off.
2. Add the onions, garlic, stewed tomacloves, garlic powder and tomato paste. (I have found that if you leave the stewed tomacloves in the can and take a pair of kitchen scissors to cut them it makes the job much easier and a lot less messy.)
3. Cook for 10 minutes.
4. Add enough water to rinse out cans.
5. Add the cream to beans in about 3 to 4 more cups water.
6. Add chili powder, salt and pepper to taste.

*Serve with crackers or rice.*

# Crawfish Bisque

**Stuffing Ingredients::**
2 lb Crawfish
2/3 Cup Celery, Chopped Fine
1 Cup Onions, Chopped Fine
3 or 4 Cloves Garlic, Minced
2 Tbsp Parsley, Chopped
2 tsp Creole Seasoning (pg 3)
½ Cup Green Onions, Chopped
4 Eggs, Separated
5 to 6 Slices Stale French Bread
½ Cup Cooking Oil

**Directions:**
1. Soak the stale French bread in water. When bread is soft squeeze out and set aside.
2. Separate the crawfish heads from the tails. Reserve heads to the side.
3. Mix the celery, onions, garlic, parsley, Creole seasoning, green onions, soaked French bread and the meat from the crawfish tails in a large bowl
4. Chill the crawfish mix for 3 to 4 hours to allow the seasonings to "mellow".
5. Clean the reserved crawfish heads and stuff with the mix. If you don't want to stuff the heads you can make little balls of the mix about the size of your little finger, set aside.
6. Beat the egg whites until very stiff and dip the stuffed crawfish heads (or rolled crawfish balls) into the egg whites.
7. Fry in oil until browned. Set aside.

**Bisque Ingredients:**
½ Cup Cooking Oil
1 Cup Flour
1 Cup Onions, Chopped Fine
1 Cup Celery, Chopped Fine
2 ¼ tsp Creole Seasoning
2-4 Cloves Garlic, Chopped Fine
2 ½ to 3 Qt Water ½ Cup Green Onions, Chopped Fine
½ Cup Parsley Crawfish Heads or Balls

**Directions:**
1. Is in a heavy skillet make a roux .
2. Add the onions celery and garlic, cook for about 10 minutes.
3. Place this mixture in a rather large stock or soup pot; add the water, green onions, Creole seasoning and the fried crawfish heads or falls from before.
4. Simmer on low heat for 45 minutes to an hour.
5. Add parsley and simmer for 10 to 15 minutes more.
6. Serve over hot rice, add a salad and hot bread.

*Serves 8*

# Crawfish Stew

**Ingredients:**
3 lb Crawfish Tails, Frozen
1 Large Onion Chopped
2 Cloves Garlic, Chopped
1 Stem Celery, Chopped
⅔ Cup Flour
⅔ Cup Shortening
4 Cups Water
Salt, red and/or black pepper to Taste

**Directions:**
1. Wash crawfish and if needed peel the tails.
2. Make a roux.
3. Add the onions, garlic and celery. Cook on medium heat until the onions are tender; about 10 minutes.
4. Add crawfish and water; simmer until the crawfish are done (they will turn pink), about 20 minutes.

*Serve with hot rice.*
*Serves 6 to 8*

Add a tossed salad and homemade bread;
you'll think you died and went to heaven!

# Daddy's Chicken and Okra Gumbo

**Ingredients:**
4 Cloves Garlic, Chopped Fine
¼ Cup Chopped Celery
1 Tbsp "Kitchen Bouquet"
2 ½ Quarts Water
4 Green Onions, Chopped
½ Cup Flour
3 Cups Fresh Okra, Slice
1 ½ Cup Oil
½ Cup Green Bell Pepper, Chopped
1 Chicken
1 Can Stewed Tomacloves, Seasoned

**Directions:**
1. In 1 cup of oil fry the okra to remove all the slime. (Do not use an iron pot/pan for this as it will turn the okra black!)
2. Make a roux. When the flour is dark enough add the green onions, green peppers, celery and garlic. Mix well stirring often.
3. Fry the chicken pieces and add to the pot with water.
4. Cook on low heat for 1 hour. If the gravy is not dark enough add a little more "kitchen bouquet".
5. Add the fried okra and stewed tomacloves, cook for 15 minutes.
6. If the gravy is too thin add the cornstarch mixed with a little cold water. If too thick add hot water.

*Serve hot and over rice*
*Makes 8 to 10 servings*

# Daddy's Potato Salad

**Ingredients:**
6 -8 Irish Potacloves 2
Slices Bacon, Cooked
1 Small Onion Chopped
3 Tbsp Vinegar
Bacon Drippings
4 Tbsp Yellow Mustard
2 Tsp Fresh Parsley, Chopped
4 - 5 Green Onions, Chopped
4 Eggs, Hardboiled
Salt and Pepper to Taste

**Directions:**
1. Peel and chop the potacloves; and a pot cook the potacloves and have just tender. Do not overcook or they will be too mushy.
2. Drain potacloves well and set aside.
3. Cook the bacon until done, crumbled bacon and set aside. Save the bacon drippings.
4. Add the onions to the bacon drippings and cook for 5 minutes.
5. Mix the crumbled bacon, chopped eggs, onions and drippings and with the potacloves.
6. Mix them into their annual of master together and add to potacloves.
7. Add the salt, pepper, parsley and the green onions; mix lightly.

*Serve hot or cold.*
*Serves 6.*

# ÉTOUFFÉE

**Ingredients:**
½ Cup Oil
½ Cup Flour
1 Large Onion, Chopped
½ Cup Celery, Chopped
1 - 6 oz Can Tomato Paste
5 to 6 Cups Water
1 lb Crawfish Tails*
1 tsp Creole Seasoning
1 Bay Leaf
4 Tbsp Parsley, Fresh
4 Cloves Garlic, Chopped
½ Cup Green Bell Pepper, Chopped

**Directions:**
1. Make a roux.
2. Add onions, green peppers and celery; allow to cook until tender, about 10 minutes.
3. Slowly add parsley, garlic, bay leaf, tomato paste and hot water; let cook for about 10 minutes, stirring occasionally.
4. Add the crawfish and Creole seasoning and simmer on very low heat for another 15–30 minutes. The crawfish (*or shrimp) should be pink in color.

*Crab meat or shrimp can be substituted for the crawfish.*
*Serve hot over rice.*
*Serves 6*

# Grandma Adams's Corn Soup

**Ingredients:**
½ Tbsp Parsley, Chopped
1 Can Whole Corn
2 qt Water
5 Ears Corn, Fresh
3 tsp Creole Seasoning
2 Tbsp Shortening
1 Can Tomacloves, Stewed
1 Onion, Chopped
2 Cloves Garlic, Chopped
4 Green Onions
2 Lb Shrimp Cleaned & Divined
4 Potacloves, Cut Into 1 Inch Cubes

**Directions:**
1. In a pan melt shortening, fry the fresh corn.
2. Add the onions, garlic, Creole seasoning, water, potacloves and the tomacloves.
3. Let cook very slowly.
4. Add the shrimp, parsley, and green onions.
5. Cook until the shrimp is paying, about 15 minutes. Make sure the potacloves are done, but not mushy.
6. Add the canned corn while stirring well.

*Serves about 6 to 8.*

# Mae's Corn Soup

**Ingredients:**
1 Lb Shrimp Peeled & Divined
¼ Cup Parsley, Chopped
½ Cup Onion, Chopped
½ Cup Celery, Chopped
½ Cup Green Onions, Chopped
8 Cups of Water
3 Cans Whole Corn with Liquid
4 Potacloves, Cut
Salt and Pepper to Taste
¾ Cup Flour
2 Cans Creamed Corn
¾ Cup Oil
1 Can Tomato Paste + 3 Cans Water
½ Cup Green Bell Pepper, Chopped

**Directions:**
1. In a large soup pot make a roux sauté until golden brown.
2. Add onions bell pepper and celery; cook about 10 minutes or until tender.
3. Add tomato paste, cans of water, hot water and potacloves; cook for about 30 minutes.
4. Add cans of corn, shrimp, green onions and parsley.
5. Cook until shrimp are pink and potacloves are tender, stirring well.
6. Season to taste with salt and pepper.

*Makes about 3 ½ quarts.*

# Potato Soup

**Ingredients:**
4 Large White Potacloves
1 Large Onion, Chopped
1 Stick Butter (or Oleo)
3 Tbsp Green Onions, Chopped
1 Cup Milk 8 oz Potacloves, Instant
3 Tbsp Fresh Parsley, Chopped
Salt & Pepper to Taste
6 Cups Water
½ Cup Ham, Boiled, Cut In 1 Inch Chunks

**Directions:**
1. In large saucepan and add the water in the potacloves.
2. Cook until potacloves are almost tender, add the ham.
3. Stir in the onions, green onions, parsley, milk, butter (or oleo) and instant potato flakes.
4. Add salt and pepper to taste; stir until well blended.

*Serves 5 to 6*

## Salad Dressing I

**Ingredients:**
½ Cup Olive Oil
½ Cup Honey
¼ tsp Dry Mustard
½ Cup Apple Cider Vinegar

**Directions:**
1. Mix all ingredients well.

## Salad Dressing II

**Ingredients:**
½ Cup Olive Oil
1 tsp Salt
2 Tbsp Honey
3 Tbsp Apple Cider Vinegar

**Directions:**
1. Mix all ingredients well.

# Shrimp and Okra Gumbo

**Ingredients:**
2 lb Shrimp
½ Cup Flour
½ Cup Oil
½ Cup Bell Pepper, Chopped
½ Cup Onion, Chopped
¼ Cup Parsley, Chopped
2 Cloves Garlic, Chopped
3 qt Water
½ Cup Celery, Chopped
3 Green Onions, Chopped
1 Tbsp Creole Seasoning
1 Can Tomacloves, Stewed
2 - 3 Cups Okra, Fresh or Frozen, Sliced

**Directions:**
1. In a heavy pot heat the oil and add the okra. Stir often, frying out all the slime. (Do not use an iron pot/pan for this as it will turn the okra black!)
2. Make a roux and cook until dark brown and pour into 5 quart stock pot.
3. Add the onions, bell pepper, celery, garlic, green onions and parsley. Cook until soft.
4. Add the okra and a can of stewed tomacloves, including liquid, and water; stir well cooking for 15–20 minutes on medium heat.
5. Add the shrimp and cook on medium about 35 minutes or until the shrimp turns pink.
6. Remove from heat and allow to cool for 15 minutes before serving.

*Serve over hot rice*
*Makes eight servings*

# Spinach Salad

**Ingredients:**
1 Bunch Fresh Spinach
1 Tomato
2 Stalks Celery, Chopped
½ Medium Red Onion
1 Yellow Bell Pepper
1 Green Bell Pepper
1 Clove Garlic, Chopped
Salt and Pepper to Taste
Italian Salad Dressing

**Directions:**
1. Wash spinach well to remove any dirt and take off all stems draining well.
2. Slice yellow and green bell peppers into long strips.
3. Slice red onion into thin slices and separate the rings.
4. Chop tomacloves very fine.
5. Mix celery, green and yellow bell peppers, tomato, red onion, garlic, salt and pepper into large bowl. Toss well and chill.
6. Before serving add Italian salad dressing and toss again.

*Serves 4 to 5*

# Three Bean Salad

**Ingredients:**
1-1 lb Can Green Beans
1-1 lb Can Yellow Wax Beans
1-1 lb. Can Red Kidney Beans
½ Green Bell Pepper, Chopped
3 Green Onions, Chopped
1 Cup Celery, Chopped
½ Red Onion, Sliced (Separate Rings)
Salt & Pepper to Taste

**Directions:**
1. Combine all the vegetables, beans and add the salt, pepper and dressing.
2. Chill for 6 to 8 hours.

# Vegetable Soup with Barley

**Ingredients:**
8-9 Cups Water
3 Carrots, Sliced
½ tsp Sweet Basil
½ - ¾ Cup Barley
1 Large Onion, Cut
2 Beef Bouillon Cubes
1 Cup Celery, Chopped
2 Cloves Garlic, Chopped
1-6 oz Can Tomato Paste
1 lb Beef, Cut Into 1"Pieces
½ Cup Alphabet Pasta
¼ Cup Green Onion, Chopped
¼ Cup Fresh Parsley, Chopped
1-1 lb Bag Frozen Soup Vegetables

**Directions:**
1. Brown beef in skillet.
2. Add onions and garlic, cook and 10 minutes or until the onions are tender.
3. Stir in water, sweet basil, celery, carrots, beef bouillon cube, fresh parsley, tomato paste and barley. Cover and bring to a boil.
4. Reduce heat to simmer and cook for 1 hour stirring occasionally.
5. If soup is too thick add more water
6. Add the frozen vegetables and alphabet pasta, cook 15 more minutes.

*Makes 12 to 14 cups*

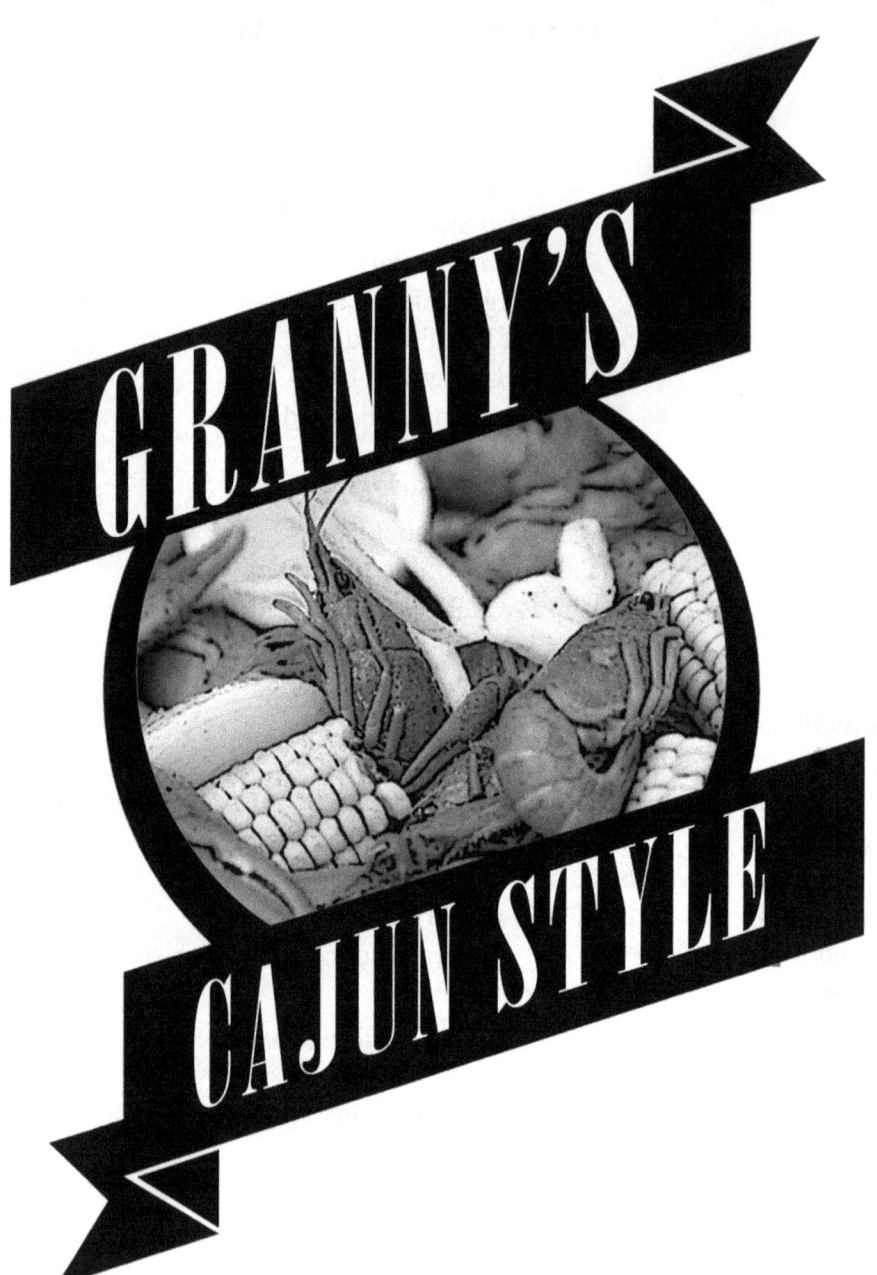

# Apples and Pork Chops

**Ingredients:**
6 Pork Chops, Center Cut
2 Red Apples (Rome or Winesap)
⅓ tsp Cinnamon
1 Tbsp Butter
2 Tbsp Cooking Oil Creole Seasoning to Taste

**Directions:**
1. Preheat oven to 350°.
2. Wash and core the apples, but do NOT peel them.
3. Cut the apples into ½ inch circles and set aside.
4. Season the pork chops with Creole seasoning and brown in a skillet with the cooking oil.
5. Place browned pork chops into a buttered casserole dish.
6. Melt the butter on medium heat and sauté the apples until tender.
7. Place one apple ring on each pork chop.
8. Sprinkle cinnamon on each apple slice.
9. Cover and bake for 25-30 minutes.

*Serves 6*

# Bulk Sicilian Sweet Sausage

**Ingredients:**
5 pounds pork butt or pork shoulder (cut into 1" pieces)
2 ½ teaspoons salt
3 teaspoons fennel seeds
2 ½ teaspoons black or white pepper
3 cloves garlic chopped fine
1 teaspoon sweet basil
¼ cup fresh parsley chopped 1 teaspoon cayenne pepper

**Directions:**
1. Grind the meat and the fat together.
2. Mix all the seasonings and the herbs together, sprinkle over meat.
3. Using your hands or a very large spoon, mix everything together.
4. Chill about 1 hour.
5. Mix again.
6. Make a test patty, cook in a little shortening, turn over and cook on the other side until brown and the liquid juices are clear.
7. Taste to see if the seasoning are right to your own liking., If more salt or pepper is need, add now.
8. Make into patties or use for stuffing vegetables or for my "Stir Fry" or make into links, your choice.

*Makes 5 pounds*

# Cajun Green Beans

**Ingredients:**
2 to 3 pounds fresh green beans
6 large red new potacloves
1 pond ham
1 large onion chopped
2 to 3 tablespoons oil

**Directions:**
1. Prepare the green beans by snapping and removing both ends and strings.
2. Rinse and drain well.
3. Scrub the potacloves until all the dirt had been removed. Cut the potacloves into ¼ pieces making all the pieces about the same size.
4. Heat the oil in a heavy pot with a tight fitting lid.
5. Place the washed beans in the pot with the hot oil. Cook on medium heat for about 10 minutes. Stir often to keep from sticking.
6. Add the potacloves and the chopped onions, stir and cover with tight fitting lid. Turn fire/heat down as low as it can go.
7. Cook 10 minutes, then stir, cook and stir until the potacloves are almost tender.
8. Add ham and cook until the potacloves and beans are done.

*Serves 6 to 8*

# Cajun Squash

**Ingredients:**
2 Cloves garlic
(Salt and black pepper to taste)
2 Zucchini medium to large sliced
4 small yellow crooked neck squash
2 white summer squash
1 medium onion sliced
4 green onions (Shallots - both tops and bottoms)
¼ cup fresh chopped parsley
¼ teaspoon sweet basil
1 can seasoned stewed tomacloves
½ green pepper
1 pound sausage (fresh or smoked)
3 Tablespoons butter

**Directions:**
1. Wash the three different squashes (if they are all young and tender there is no need to peel them) Slice them up.
2. If you are using fresh sausage to cook them in a little water then brown. Cut them into 1" links. If you are using smoked sausage there is no need to cook them first; just cut them into 1" links.
3. Brown onions, green onions, parsley, green peppers in the better.
4. Add all 3 squashes, cook on medium heat for about 10 minutes.
5. Add the sausages.
6. Add the can of stewed tomacloves.
7. Add the garlic, salt and pepper.
8. Cook on low heat until the squash is tender.

*Serves 6*

# Corn Casserole

**Ingredients:**
1 ½ pound fresh country sausage (Bulk)
1 large can cream corn
1 large onion chopped
1 toe garlic
½ green bell pepper chopped
2 green onions
2 Tablespoons fresh parsley chopped
3-4 Tablespoons oil
2 eggs well beaten
½ cup yellow corn meal
½ to ¾ cup milk

**Directions:**
1. Saute the onion, green onions, bell pepper, garlic in the heated oil.
2. Add the bulk sausage (if you can buy or make bulk sausage, remove the meat from the casings.)
3. Cook for about 15 minutes.
4. Add corn, yellow corn meal, milk, and parsley, mix well.
5. Add the well beaten eggs mix well.
6. Pour into a buttered casserole dish.
7. Bake in a preheated oven 350° F for about 30 to 35 minutes.

If it is to dry add a little more milk,
if it is to wet add a little more cornmeal.

*Serves 6*

# Creole Red Rice—Jambalaya

**Ingredients:**
4 cups cooked long grain rice
1 pound smoke sausage or Andouille
2 green peppers chopped
4 green onions chopped
2 cloves garlic chopped
2 Tablespoon parsley chopped
1 can whole yellow corn (liquid and all)
1 can tomato paste
2 Tablespoons cooking oil

**Directions:**
1. The rice should be already cooked before cooking the jambalaya (I always use an electric rice cooker, the rice is cooking while I am cooking the rest of the ingredients.)
2. In a large 5 quart pot, place the oil when it is hot add the onions. Cook until they begin to brown.
3. Add the tomato paste, chopped green peppers, garlic, parsley and the meat.
4. Stir well, now add some hot water simmer about 30 minutes.
5. Add the corn and the liquid, stirring well.
6. Add the corn and the liquid, stirring well.
7. Turn down the heat as low as it will go and cook about 30 minutes, stirring every now and then to be sure it is not sticking.
8. Cook until all the liquid is cooked down and the meat is done.

*Serves 8 to 9*

# CREOLE SAUSAGE

**Ingredients:**
2 pounds fresh leans pork butt
2 pounds beef
1 pound pork fat
1 large onion
1 teaspoon cayenne pepper
1 teaspoon ground cloves
¼ teaspoon allspice
½ teaspoon nutmeg
½ teaspoon anise
3 teaspoons salt
2 to 3 cloves garlic chopped fine
½ teaspoon fresh parsley chopped fine
¼ teaspoon thyme crushed

**Directions:**
1. In a meat grinder with the course blade grind the beef the pork and the fat. SEPARATELY.
2. Add all the seasonings together and sprinkle on the meat.
3. Knead the seasoning into the meat using a large spoon. (use your hands if you wish, works for me)
4. Now chill this mixture for about 1 hour.
5. Mix again, and then place the meat mixture through the grinder using the fine blade.
6. Test the sausage by making 1 patty, cook it in shorting until very born on both sides.
7. Taste to see if there is enough salt and pepper to your taste, if not now is the time to add more.
8. Stuff into prepared casings or make into parries.
9. Allow the sausage to "Mellow"—set up.

*Makes 5 pounds*

# Fresh Greens

**Ingredients:**
1 bunch fresh mustard greens
1 bunch turnips tops and bottoms
1 large onion chopped medium fine
1 pound salt pork or pickled port
Water

**Directions:**
1. Clean and wash the vegetables (wash the greens about three times to get all the dirt off).
2. Chop the greens into small pieces.
3. Cut the white part of the turnips into small pieces.
4. Add a little water about 1 cup to the vegetables.
5. Add the onions and the meat to the pot.
6. Add salt and pepper.
7. As the greens cook add a little water if needed to keep from burning.
8. When all is tender turn off the heat and keep warm until ready to serve.
9. Using a spotted spoon (A spoon with holes in it) remove the meat and the vegetables.
10. Pass the apple cider vinegar allowing each person to use what they want.
11. Serve with hot homemade core bread.

*Serves 4 to 6*

# Fresh Pork Sausage Country Style

**Ingredients:**
3 pounds ground pork ( fat and lean)
1 ½ teaspoon of Creole Seasoning or mix to your taste - (Garlic powder and onion powder about 2 teaspoons each in addition)
4 Tablespoons fresh parsley chopped
½ teaspoon stage (crushed between the fingers)
½ teaspoon nutmeg
¼ teaspoon summer savor
¼ cup fresh green onions chopped both tops and bottoms

**Directions:**
1. Grind the fat and lean together (or maybe purchased from meat market together).
2. Mix all the seasons into a small dish, mix well.
3. With a teaspoon, sprinkle all the Creole seasons over the meat and stir well.
4. Chill at lease 2 hours.
5. Make a patty, cook it until its done, taste to see if more seasoning is needed, adjust if necessary.
6. Make into patties. (I use a hamburger press)
7. If made into links the sausage links may be pan fried or may be grilled.
8. The sausage meat may be used for stuffing vegetables or in stir frying.
9. The sausage may also be smoked, however, omit the green onions and add finely chopped white onions in their place.

# Italian Zucchini Casserole

**Ingredients:**
5 medium size zucchini
½ cup onion chopped 1 egg beaten
1 ½ pounds fresh Italian bulk sausage
Seasoned bread crumbs
¼ cup green onions (tops and bottoms) chopped
½ stick butter or oleo
Salt and pepper to taste
Garlic powder to taste
½ cup hot water
1 beef bouillon cube

**Directions:**
1. Wash and cut off the stem and the blossom ends from the zucchini.
2. Cut the zucchini into 1/8".
3. Brown the sausage in 3 Tablespoons oil until brown.
4. Add the zucchini, salt, pepper, garlic powder, and green onions cook about 10 minutes.
5. Add beaten egg and some bread crumbs (start with about ½ cup of crumbs).
6. Place into a casserole dish, sprinkle with crumbs and place little parts of butter on top.
7. Microwave on 7 power about 25 minutes or place in a preheated oven 300° F for 40 to 50 minutes.

If the dish is to wet add more crumbs, if it is to dry add more water.

# Ma's Cajun Stir-Fry

**Ingredients:**
6 ounces Kikkoman stir-fry sauce
2 packages sun bird beef and broccoli sauce mix
2 ¼ cups water
2 Tablespoons olive oil
1 ½ pounds fresh country sausage (cut into 1" pieces)
8 ounces fresh mushrooms sliced
4 carrots (cut thin into circles)
4 stems celery (cut on an angle)
1 large onion (cut half, then sliced thin)
3 cloves garlic shopped
1 bag frozen bell peppers (do not thaw out)
6 stems parsley cut fine
6 green onions or shallots cut up not fine
Salt and pepper to taste

PLACE EACH VEGETABLE IN A SEPARATE CONTAINER AND CHILL UNTIL READY TO USE.

**Directions:**
1. Place the oil onto a wok or a very large pot reheat the oil to about 350° F.
2. Place the cut up sausage into the oil and cook about 5 minutes until lightly brown.
3. Add the onions and cook about 5 minutes.
4. Add the carrots, celery, garlic, parsley, and cook about 3 to 5 minutes more.
5. Mushrooms, salt and pepper come next.
6. Add the stir fry sauce, and the broccoli sauce with the water, blend well.
7. Simmer for 5 to 8 minutes turn off the heat, let stand for about 5 minutes.

Serve with home made Egg Rolls
*Serves 6 to 8*

# Ma's Red Beans and Rice

**Ingredients:**
1 pound dry red kidney beans
1 pound ham, sausage or Anduoulli cut into 1" pieces
1 large onion chopped fine
¼ cup cooking oil
½ green pepper chopped
4 to 6 green onions shopped
4 stems of parsley chopped
3 cloves of garlic
Salt and pepper to taste

**Directions:**
1. Pick over the beans, removing any rocks or bad beans.
2. Wash and drain the beans.
3. Cover with water and soak over night.
4. Next day drain the beans and rinse again (I rinse them about 3 times)
5. Add the beans onions, green peppers, garlic, green onions, and parsley.
6. Add about 2 quarts water adding when needed.
7. Cook about 1 hour, check to be sure there is enough water to cover the beans, bring to a rolling boil.
8. Add meat and the Creole Seasoning, salt and pepper.
9. Add the cooking oil, let simmer about 40 to 50 minutes more, until creamy. (Smash a few beans against the pot to make sure they are tender)

THE BEANS SHOULD BE CREAMY NOT BROKEN UP.

Serve over hot rice
*Serves 8 to 10*

# Pork Chop Casserole

**Ingredients:**
Salt and pepper to taste
4 center pork chops
½ cups raw long grain rice
1 can 10 ¾ ounces beef gravy
½ cup water (rinse out can)
4 medium carrots cut into 1 ½" pieces
2 medium onions sliced.

**Directions:**
1. Preheat oven to 350° F.
2. Trim off all the fat from the pork chops.
3. Sprinkle the salt and pepper.
4. Brown the chops on both sides (In 2 Tablespoons of cooking oil).
5 Remove the meat to a 2 quart casserole dish.
6. Add the rice to the pan drippings, stirring until nice and brown.
7. Stir in the beef gravy, water, salt and a little pepper.
8. Place the onions on top of the meat and pour the gravy mixture over the chops.
9. Cover and bake for 1 hour or until rice is done.

*Serves 4*

# Red Beans A LA Maw Maw Edie Adams

**Ingredients:**
1 jar 32 ounces Ragu tomato sauce
1 pound red beans
1 pound pickle pork shoulder
2 carrots chopped very fine
1 small onion chopped
2 to 4 cloves garlic chopped fine (depending upon the side of the cloves)
3 stems of celery chopped fine
3 bay leaves (leave whole)
1 Tablespoon Louisiana Hot sauce
1/8 cup parsley chopped

**Directions:**
1. Soak the beans about 4 hours, drain off all the water, rinse a few times
2. Add the rest of the ingredients
3. Cook down on medium heat until the beads are tender about 3 to 4 hours
4. Serve over hot cook rice

*Serves 7 to 8*

# Sauerkraut Pork

**Ingredients:**
1 Tablespoon cooking oil
1 medium onion chopped
2 pounds sauerkraut (drained and rinsed)
¼ teaspoon careaway seeds
1 to 2 teaspoon sugar
2 pounds pork ribs, or pork shoulder or pork chops
1 quart water

**Directions:**
1. Heat the oil, add the onions cook until tender about 10 minutes
2. In a very large pot add ½ the sauerkraut, sprinkle ½ the onions (do the same thing make two layers)
3. On the top of the kraut, sprinkle the caraway seeds, and the sugar
4. Place the pork meat on top of the seasonings (press the meat well onto the kraut) Now pour the water over the meat.

Cover and bake in a preheated oven 350° F about 2 to 3 hours
(pork meat must be well done cook until meat is tender)

Serve Hot
*Serves 6*

# Scalloped Potacloves with Sausage

**Ingredients:**
3 Tablespoons butter
1 Pound fresh sausage links (any kind-country, Italian, etc. hot or mild)
6 large potacloves
1 can cream of celery or cream of mushroom soup
3 can pet milk
Dash of cayenne pepper
Salt and pepper to taste
1 onion thinly sliced
1 ½ Tablespoon corn starch

**Directions:**
1. In a skillet or wok cook the sausage in just enough water to cover the bottom of the pan. When the sausage is light brown remove them from the pan, and set aside. Cut into pieces.
2. Wash the potacloves pare and slice them into think slices.
3. Mix in the cream soup with some of the milk. Add the corn starch to the milk to make a paste.
4. Add the butter and cook on medium hear until the mixture thickens.
5. Add the salt pepper and the cayenne.
6. In a buttered casserole layer the potacloves and then the sausage, then the onions and then the sauce. (being and end with the sausage.)
7. Bake in a hot oven 400° F for 30 minutes covered then uncovered for 15 to 20 minutes more.

*Serves 6*

## SMOKED SAUSAGE ALFREDO

**Ingredients:**
sweet basil to taste
2 cups of Rotini or home made noodles
1 pound smoked sausage sliced
1 bunch broccoli
1 can corn ( Mexican style)
1 small onion chopped
Salt and pepper to taste
2 packages Alfredo sauce mix

**Directions:**
1. Cook the noodles in boiling water until tender about 8 to 10 minutes
2. Cook the sauce following the package directions.
3. Clean the broccoli (use the flower sections)
4. Add the Mexican corn, stir.
5. Add the smoke sausage, let it all simmer for about 15 to 20 minutes
6. Add the cooked noodles to the sausage mixture

Sweet Italian sausage, fresh country sausage or smoked ham may also be used in place of the smoke sausage.
*Makes 5 to 6 servings*

## Stuffed Artichokes

**Ingredients:**
4 large artichokes
3 cups Italian bread crumbs
1 ¼ cups Romano Cheese grated
1 ¼ cups Parmesan Cheese grated
Mozzarella cheese cut into cubs
3 cloves garlic chopped
1 large onion 2 green onions (shallots - both tops and bottoms)
1 cup olive oil
Pinch salt
Pinch black pepper
1 lemon (cut into slices)
1 pound Italian style sausage
1 egg

**Directions:**
1. Trim off the tops of the artichokes using a kitchen scissors.
2. Cut off the lower stems.
3. Wash well, and bar boil the artichokes, drain well.
4. Spread the leaves open and set aside.
5. Add all the other ingredients together except the lemon slices and the olive oil.
6. Sprinkle the mixture into the leaves tapping the artichoke on the table to help settle the mixture better.
7. Place into a large banking pan with 1 inch water, put a little oil into the leaves. Add cubes of butter and 1 slice of lemon to each choke.
8. Bake 350° F for 30 minutes.

Shrimp, ham, crawfish, or sausage may be cooked
and added to the crumb mix.

*Serves 4*

# Stuffed Pork Chops

**Ingredients:**
6 center pork chops cut 1 ½" thick
(make a pocket in each one do not butterfly)
Pam spray
½ to ¾ pound fresh sausage, crawfish, ground turkey, shrimp
(take your pick.)
1 Tablespoon chopped onion
1 tablespoon green onion chopped
½ sweet basil dried and crushed
¼ cup seasoned bread crumbs
¼ cup water
1 beaten egg
Garlic powder, salt, pepper, to taste
¼ teaspoon fennel seed if you wish.

**Directions:**
1. Preheat oven 375° F
2. Cook the sausage (etc) remove from skillet, place into a pot.
3. Cook the chopped onion, green onion and the sweet basil, in the meat drippings.
4. Add the cooked sausage (etc) water egg add salt, pepper. Add the fennel seeds if you wish.
5. Add the bread crumbs stir well. If to dry add a little more water, if to wet add a little more bread crumbs.
6. Stuff the pork chops.
7. Melt the butter and the garlic powder, baste the chops.
8. Spray the pan with Pam.
9. Place the chops into the baking pan. Place the pan into the preheated oven.
10. Baste with the butter often.
11. Cook for about 45 minutes.

# Turnips and Irish Potacloves

**Ingredients:**
4 to 5 medium turnips
4 medium potacloves
4 slices bacon
¼ onion chopped
4 tablespoon flour
Salt and pepper to taste

**Directions:**
1. Peel and wash the turnips and the potacloves cut into circles.
2. Cook the turnips and the potacloves in boiling water.
3. In a skillet, cook the bacon, remove the bacon from the pan (save drippings).
4. Heat the beacon drippings add the flour brown until golden in color add the onions stir well.
5. Watch closely so that it does not burn.
6. Stir the onion mixture into the potacloves and the turnips.
7. Keep warm until ready to serve.

*3 to 4 servings*

# Zucchini and Sausage Casserole

**Ingredients:**
1 large onion chopped
2 to 4 zucchini (depending on the size)
2 pounds sweet Italian sausage (fresh bulk)
¼ cup green onion chopped
3 cloves of garlic chopped
¼ cups granted Romano Cheese
3 Tablespoons chopped fresh parsley
1 egg well beaten
Italian bread crumbs
6 ounce can tomato paste

**Directions:**
1. Boil the zucchini in enough water to cover them.
2. Cook for 10 minutes then remove from the water and dry and set aside.
3. In a heavy skillet saute the sausage until brown add the onions and the garlic and cook for 5 minutes.
4. Cut the bar boiled zucchini into slices and add to the sausage mixture.
5. Add the tomato paste stir well. Add a little water to the can to rinse it out, mix well.
6. Add cheese, parley, salt, pepper, cook for about 5 minutes. On low heat.
7. Add the beaten egg and the bread crumbs.
8. If the mixture seems to be to think add a little more water, add it slowly. If the mixture is a little to thin add a little more bread crumbs.
9. Pour into a butter casserole dish, and sprinkle a little bread crumbs over the top a cub of butter here and there.
10. Bake in a preheated oven 350° F for 30 minutes.

*Serves 6*

# Artichoke Heart Casserole

**Ingredients:**
2 Cans Artichoke Hearts
1 Lb Shrimp, Peeled & Divined
1 Large Onion, Chopped
2 Cloves Garlic, Chopped
1 Bunch Green Onions, Chopped
3 Tbsp Fresh Parsley, Chopped
1 Egg, Well Beaten
1 Cup Seasoned Bread Crumbs
½ Cup Parmesan Cheese, Grated
3 Tbsp Olive Oil
3 Tbsp Lemon Juice
Salt and Pepper to Taste

**Directions:**
1. Preheat oven to 350° F
2. Heat olive oil in skillet; add the onions, garlic and green onions. Sauté about 5 minutes.
3. Add shrimp to skillet and cook until the shrimp turn pink, about 5 minutes.
4. Drain artichoke hearts and reserve liquid.
5. Place artichoke hearts in blender and set to chop; if needed add a little liquid back in
6. Add artichoke hearts, egg, lemon juice and Parmesan cheese. Stir well, cooking until eggs are done.
7. Place in a buttered casserole dish and sprinkle bread crumbs on top.
8. Bake for 25 minutes.

*Serves 6*

# Barbeque Red Fish A La Tommy

**Ingredients:**
1 Large Red Fish
Creole Seasoning

**Directions:**
1. Cut the fish from the tail to the head.
2. Cut off the head and tail.
3. Do not remove the scales.
4. Use Creole seasoning on the meat side, not the scale side of the fish.
5. Place on hot grill.
6. Cover the meat side of barbecue sauce.
7. Cook only until the meat is dry, about 10 minutes.

*Tommy uses a gas grill, one that he can control the heat. We hope you will enjoy this as much as we do.*

# Broccoli, Rice & Shrimp Casserole

**Ingredients:**
2 lb Shrimp Peeled & Divined
½ Cup Green Onions, Chopped
1 ½ Cups Water
1 Stick Butter or Oleo
1 Onion, Chopped
½ Cup Green Pepper, Chopped
1 - 8 Oz Jar Cheese Whiz
2 Cups Instant Rice
½ Cup Celery, Chopped
Salt to Taste
Black Pepper to Taste
Cayenne Pepper to Taste
2 - 10 oz Packages Frozen Broccoli
2 Cans Cream of Mushroom Soup

**Directions:**
1. Preheat oven to 350° F

2. Cook broccoli, drain and set aside.
3. In a pan heat the butter and cook the onions, green peppers and green onions until tender, about 5 minutes.
4. Add the soup then rinse the cans with roughly ½ can of water each, mixing this in the pan as well.
5. Add celery and shrimp and cook until shrimp turns pink.
6. Add rice, salt, black pepper, cayenne pepper and cheese whiz; stir well.
7. Add the broccoli mix well and pour into a buttered casserole dish.
8. Bake about 30 minutes.

## Crawfish Pie

**Ingredients:**
2 lb Crawfish Tails
1 Stick Butter (or Oleo)
2 Cans Cream of Celery Soup*
4 to 5 Tbsp Corn Starch
1 ½ Cans Evaporated Milk
¼ Cup Parsley, Chopped
1 Large Onion, Chopped
1 tsp Creole Seasoning
¼ Cup Celery, Chopped
2 Pie Crusts
3 to 4 Cloves Garlic, Chopped Fine

**Directions:**
1. Preheat oven to 350° F.
2. In a heavy skillet (I use a black iron pot), heat the butter. Sauté the onions, garlic, parsley and celery until just limp (do not overcook).
3. Add the cream of celery soup*.
4. Mix the cornstarch with a little bit of milk to make a paste; Rinse out the two soup cans with a little milk and add to the cornstarch paste stirring slowly.
5. Slowly stir in the milk and cornstarch paste into the pot.
6. Let cook for about 10 minutes.
7. Add the crawfish tails to the pot and stir well.
8. Pour the mix into two pie shells (I use frozen ones).
9. Bake for about 30 to 35 minutes just until the crust is browned.

*Can substitute cream of shrimp soup.     Each pie makes 6 to 8 servings.

# Eggplant and Shrimp Casserole

**Ingredients:**
1 lb Shrimp*, Peeled and Divined
1 Stick Butter Or Olio
1 Large Onion, Chopped
1 Bunch Green Onions, Chopped
¼ Cup Fresh Parsley
2-3 Cloves Garlic, Chopped
¼ Cup Green Pepper, Chopped
1 Large Eggplant
2 Eggs, Well Beaten
1 Cup Seasoned Bread Crumbs

**Directions:**
1. Preheat oven to 350° F.
2. Peel and slice the eggplant; cook until tender in boiling water.
3. When the eggplant is tender drain well and mash.
4. Melt the butter into a pan; add the onions, garlic and green pepper. Cook until soft, about 5 minutes.
5. Add shrimp to the pan, cooking until the shrimp turns pink.
6. Add the mashed eggplant, beaten eggs, parsley and bread crumbs; mix well.
7. Place into a buttered casserole dish and bake for 25 to 30 minutes.

**1 pound ground beef, crawfish or ham may be used in place of shrimp.*
*Serves 6*

# French Fried Shrimp

**Ingredients:**
1 tsp Salt
1 tsp Sugar
1 Cup of Ice Water
1 Egg, Beaten
1 Cup Corn Flour or Yellow Cornmeal
2 lb Large Shrimp, Peeled & Divined

**Directions:**
1. Preheat oil in deep fryer to 350° F.
2. Combine salt, sugar, water and cornflower or yellow cornmeal in a large mixing bowl.
3. Chill the batter.
4. Wash the shrimp well; dry thoroughly.
5. When the oil is hot dip the shrimp into the chilled batter and fry until golden brown.
6. Drain shrimp on paper towels.

*Serve with hot "hush puppies", French fries or tomato ketchup; may also be made into "Po - Boy" sandwiches.*

*Serves 7 to 8*

# Seafood Pasta

**Ingredients:**
1 Bunch Green Onions, Chopped
1 lb Medium Shrimp, Peeled & Divined
1 lb Crawfish Tails
1 lb Crab Claw Meat
2 Large Onions, Chopped
2 Bell Peppers, Chopped
1 Cup Celery, Chopped
2-3 Cloves Garlic, Chopped
1 Can Cream Of Celery Soup
1-12 oz Jar Picante Sauce
4 Tbsp Oil
2 Cans Cream Of Shrimp Soup
2 Lb Spaghetti Or Fettuccine, Cooked
2 Cups Half & Half

**Directions:**
1. In a large pan heat the oil. When hot add the green peppers, onions, garlic and green onions. Sautéed vegetables on medium heat until tender, about 10 minutes.
2. Add the shrimp, crawfish tails and crab claw meat; cook about 10 minutes stirring often.
3. Add the cream of celery soup, cream of shrimp soup, half & half and picante sauce (I always rinse out the soup cans with a little water, less than a ¼ cup total).
4. Cook until the shrimp and crawfish are done and turn pink.
5. Add the cooked pasta or place the pasta on a plate and add the sauce on top.

*Serves 8 to 10*
*(or 4 hungry Cajuns after a hunting trip)*

# Shrimp Fettuccine

**Ingredients:**
2 Sticks Butter or Oleo
1 Medium Onions, Chopped
3 Stems Celery, Chopped Fine
4 Tbsp Fresh Parsley, Chopped
¼ Cup Flour
1 qt Half & Half
2 lb Shrimp, Peeled & Divined
3 Cloves Garlic, Chopped
½ Cheddar Cheese, Grated
1 tsp Sweet Basil
1 Tbsp Cooking Oil Creole
Seasoning to Taste
1 lb Fettuccine, Cooked
2 Green Bell Peppers, Chopped Fine

**Directions:**
1. In a large pot melt butter on medium heat. Add onions, green peppers and celery, cooking until tender (about 10 minutes).
2. Stir in the flour, blending well. Cook for 10 more minutes stirring often.
3. Add parsley and shrimp, cover and cook another 15 minutes, stirring often.
4. Add Half & Half, grated cheese, garlic, sweet basil and Creole seasoning.
5. Cover, reduce heat to low and let cook another 12–15 minutes, stirring often. The shrimp will be pink when it is done.
6. Add the cooked pasta or place the pasta on a plate and add the sauce on top.

*Serves 8–10*

# Shrimp Pie

**Ingredients:**
1 lb Shrimp, Cooked
½ Stick Butter
1 Cup Whole Milk
3 Eggs, Well Beaten
1 Cup Celery, Chopped Very Fine
3-4 Slices Stale French Bread
2 Cloves Garlic, Chopped Very Fine
½ Cup Fresh Parsley, Chopped Fine
1 Pinch Rosemary
1 Pinch Thyme
1 Pinch Mace
1 Pinch Nutmeg
¼ Cup Green Onions, Chopped Very Fine
1 Cup Onions, Chopped Very Fine

**Directions:**
1. Preheat oven to 350° F.
2. Soak the stale French bread in milk until soft, then squeeze out and set aside. Reserve the milk.
3. In a malt butter and sauté the celery, onions, and green onions for 5 to 8 minutes, until tender.
4. Add the bread to the pan and stir well.
5. Add the shrimp and eggs to the pan, stirring well.
6. Add some of the reserved milk, stir well and cook for another 5 minutes. The mixture should look like a thick pudding.
7. Pour the mixture into a pie crust.
8. Bake for 20 minutes, or until golden brown.

*Makes 1 pie*

## Smothered Corn with Shrimp

**Ingredients:**
3 Cans Whole Kernel Corn or 1 Lb Frozen Corn
1 Large Onion, Chopped
1 lb Shrimp, Peeled & Divined
4 Tbsp Butter
¼ Cup Fresh Parsley, Chopped
½ Cup Green Bell Pepper, Chopped
2 Cups Water

**Directions:**
1. In a large sauce pan melt the butter on medium heat and sauté the onions and bell pepper until tender.
2. Add the corn and parsley to the pan, cook for another 15 minutes on medium heat.
3. Stir the shrimp and water into the pan and cook for 15 more minutes, the shrimp will turn pink when done.

*Serves 4–6*

# Stuffed Crabs I

**Ingredients:**
½ Cup Celery, Chopped
½ Cup Green Onions, Chopped
2 Cloves Garlic, Chopped Fine
¼ Cup Butter or Oleo
2 Tbsp Fresh Parsley, Chopped
1 lb Crab Meat
4 - 6 Crab Shells
½ Cup Bread Crumbs, Buttered
Creole Seasoning to Taste
Eggs, Beaten
1 ½ Cups Bread Crumbs, Seasoned

**Directions:**
1. Preheat oven to 350° F.
2. In a saucepan melt the butter over low heat and sauté the celery, green onions and garlic.
3. Add the crab meat, parsley, egg and bread crumbs, stir well.
4. Add Creole seasoning to taste and mix again. If the mixture is too wet add more bread crumbs, if the mixture is too dry and add more water.
5. Stuff the crab shells with this mixture.
6. Bake for 15 minutes or until the tops of the crabs are brown.

*This stuffing may also be used for red fish or flounder before baking.

*Stuffs 4 to 6 shells*

# Stuffed Crabs II

**Ingredients:**
1 lb Crab Meat
3 Eggs, Beaten
1 Stick Butter or Oleo
1 Medium Onion, Chopped Fine
1 Stem Celery, Chopped Fine
¼ Cup Fresh Parsley, Chopped
¼ Cup Green Onions, Chopped
4 Cloves Garlic, Chopped Fine
2 Cups Bread Crumbs
Seasoned Creole Seasoning to Taste
8 - 10 Crab Shells

**Directions:**
1. Preheat oven to 350° F.
2. Picture the crab meat to remove any shells, and set aside.
3. In a 10 melt the butter on medium heat and sauté the onions, celery, green onions and parsley for about 5 to 7 minutes.
4. Add the eggs, mixing well and reduce heat to low.
5. Add the bread crumbs and Creole seasoning staring well the mixture will be sticky.
6. Stuff the crab shells with this mixture.
7. Bake for 15 to 18 minutes or until the tops are brown.

*Stuffs 8 to 10 shells*

# Stuffed Mirliton (Vegetable Pear)

The Mirliton is a member of the squash family. It grows on a vine easily in back yards and is a light green color. It has the shape of a pear, hence the name "vegetable pear".

**Ingredients:**
3 Mirlitons
1 Green Bell Pepper, Chopped
1 Large Onion, Chopped
½ Cup Fresh Parsley, Chopped
2 Cloves Garlic, Chopped Fine
1 lb Shrimp, Peeled & Divined
1 Egg
1 Cup Seasoned Bread Crumbs
1 Stick Butter or oleo
4 Green Onions, Chopped
Creole Seasoning to Taste

**Directions:**
1. Preheat oven to 350° F.
2. Wash and boil the mirlitons hold, when fork tender remove from water and cool.
3. When cool cut the mirlitons in half and carefully scoop out the centers, reserve the shells.
4. Mash the mirlitons in a mixing bowl and set aside.
5. In a pan heat the butter and add the mashed mirlitons, onions, bell pepper, garlic and parsley; cook until the onions are just tender, about 5 minutes.
6. Add shrimp to the pan and cook until done, about 15 to 20 minutes; they will turn pink when done.
7. Stir the eggs and bread crumbs into the mixture with the Creole seasoning and allow to cook for about 10 more minutes.
8. Fill the reserved mirliton shells with the stuffing and bake for 25 minutes.

*Serves 6*

# Corn Beef Hash

**Ingredients:**
1 can corn beef or 1 pound corned beef chopped
2 Tablespoons butter or oleo
5 to 6 potacloves (depending on the size)
1 cup milk
½ teaspoon black or white pepper
1 Tablespoon grated onion

**Directions:**
1. Boil the peeled potatoes, mix with the corned beef.
2. Add the onions, butter, milk and the pepper.
3. Place in a buttered dish and microwave about 10 minutes on 7 power (be sure to cover the dish with wax paper, paper towel or glass cover.)

*Serves 4 to 5*

# Corn Beef and Cabbage

**Ingredients:**
3 to 5 pounds corn beef
1 large head of cabbage
4 large Irish potacloves
2 large onions
Pickling spice
2 carrots (optional)

**Directions:**
1. Cover the corn beef with water, and boil until almost tender. About 2 to 3 hours, remove the corn beef from the water.
2. Add the cut potacloves and the onions and cook for about 10 minutes.
3. Add the cabbage to the pot, sliced the corn beef and add it to the pot as well.
4. Cook until the cabbage, potacloves, and the corn beef are all tender.
*If you are adding carrots to the pot, add them at the same time as you are putting the potacloves and the cabbage. Cook same amount of time.

This dish is always served on New Years Day, and march 17$^{th}$.

*Serves 6 to 8*

# Dad's Hot Tamales

**Filling Ingredients:**
10 pounds beef cubed
2 tablespoons ground cumin
¼ pound ground chile powder
4 ounces ground paprika
2 full heads garlic cut very fine
2 medium onions cut fine
1 Tablespoon red hot pepper
Hot water

**Dough Ingredients:**
4 ½ pounds corn flour
*1 pound veal tallow—render out
Corn husks

**Directions:**
1. Boil the meat in the water to which you have added one onion, and a clove of garlic.
2. When the meat is tender, remove the meat and drain (save the stock to use with the dough)
3. Cut the cubed beef into smaller cubes.
4. Place the cubes into a meat grinder.
5. Heat veal tallow and render out all the fat.
6. Skim off the fat, add the meat and brown, add the onions and garlic.
7. In hot water, mix the chili powder, and spices, and mix well with the meat.
8. Cook this mixture about 10 minutes, remove from heat.
9. Dough : Into the corn flour, add the salt, the oil from the veal tallow. Add about ½ the stock that was saved from the cooked meat. Beat well with a wooden spoon.
10. Add the reminder of the stock.
11. It is very important that the dough be well beaten to make it light.
12. Dry the corn husks and on the inside spread thinly with some of the dough.
13. Add 1 ½ teaspoon of the meat mixture.
14. Roll up as you would a roll a cigarette.

15. Fold on both ends under.
16. Stack in a large steamer and cook until the dough is done—about 45 minutes to 1 hours.

My dad always used a rack to set in the bottom of a large pot. The pot was first covered with corn husks. He then world stack the hot tamales over the husks. They were stacked in a "Pyramid style".
Cover the hot tamales tightly and cook on a very low heat. Any leftovers maybe packed in freezer bags and kept in the freezer for up to 3 months.

# Dirty Rice or Cajun Dressing

**Ingredients:**
1 cup hot water
2 pounds ground beef
3 cups long grain rice (raw)
1 large onion, chopped
2 cloves garlic, chopped
1 large green onion pepper, chopped
¼ cup green onion, chopped
2 beef bouillon cubes
¼ cup parsley, chopped

**Directions:**
1. Cook the rice your way ( I use a rice cooker).
2. Dissolve the beef cubs into the hot water.
3. Cook the ground beef and drain well.
4. Add the onions, parsley, peppers, green onions, and the garlic. Cook for 10 minutes on medium heat.
5. Add the cooked rice.
6. Add the Creole seasoning.
7. Taste, add a little seasoning at a time until it is the way you want it.

*Serves 6 to 8*

# Enchiladas

### Ingredients:
1 pound ground beef
1 toe garlic chopped
1 teaspoon chili powder
1 receipt Enchilada sauce
½ to ¾ cup grated cheddar cheese
1 medium onion chopped
12 corn tortillas

**Directions:**
1. Brown the meat-drain well, add chili powder.
2. Dip the tortillas (one at a time) into the hot sauce.
3. Fill each tortilla with cheese and meat and onion.
4. Roll the filled tortilla up, placing a folded edges "down under" in a backing pan.
5. Pour the hot enchilada sauce over the rolls.
6. Sprinkle with the rest of the cheese.
7. Bake in a preheated oven 350° F for 15 minutes, or until all the cheese is melted.

# Enchilada Sauce

### Ingredients:
¼ cup oil
1 medium onion chopped
1 toe garlic chopped fine
1 8 ounce can tomato paste
2 cups water
1 teaspoon wine vinegar
1 teaspoon sugar
½ teaspoon oregano
½ teaspoon salt
Pinch of cayenne
2 teaspoons chili powder

**Directions:**
1. Heat oil in a heavy sauce pan, add the onions garlic, the water and the tomato paste.

2. Simmer for about 4 to 5 minutes.
3. Add the remaining ingredients, bring to a boil.
4. After the mixture comes to a boil, then lower the heat and simmer for about 15 to 20 minutes.

*Yield 2 cups (enough to cover 12 enchiladas)*

# Hot Stuffed Tomacloves

**Ingredients:**
½ pound ground beef
3 Tablespoons butter or oleo
1 medium onion chopped
1 cup seasoned bread crumbs
3 Tablespoons grated Parmesan cheese
1 ½ teaspoons salt
¼ teaspoon black or white pepper
6 medium to large tomacloves
3 Tablespoons fresh parsley chopped
Buttered bread crumbs for the topping
1 beaten egg

**Directions:**
1. Preheat the oven to 350° F, grease the casserole dish.
2. Melt the butter and add the onions, cook until tender about 5 minutes stirring occasionally.
3. Add the ground beef cook for 10 minutes.
4. Cut off the stem ends of the tomacloves, scoop out the pulp, be careful not to make a hole in the tomato.
5. Add the pulp and the top (chopped) to the meat mixture.
6. Add the rest of the chopped vegetables, and cook about 10 minutes.
7. Beat the egg add the meat mixture add the dry bread crumbs.
8. Cook until the egg is done, the mixture should be a little sticky.
9. Stuff each tomato with the meat mixture.

10. Place the tomatoes in a backing pan, sprinkle each tomato with the buttered crumbs toppings.
11. Add about ½" water.
12. Baked in a preheated oven 350° F for 15 minutes or just until the top of the meat mixture is slightly brown.

*Serves 6*

# Lasagna

### Ingredients:
2 pounds ground beef (lean)
2 jars 32 ounces "Prego" spaghetti sauce with mushrooms
8 ounces of fresh mushrooms sliced thin
½ Tablespoon sweet basil crushed
¼ teaspoon white or black pepper
½ cup grated Parmesan cheese
½ cup grated Romano cheese
1 ½ cups Mozzarella cheese
1 package lasagna noodles, or home made noodles
1 bay leaf crushed
¼ teaspoon basil crushed

**Directions:**
1. Place the ground beef into a 5 quart sauce pan, brown the meat and drain all the fat.
2. Add the Prego sauce, the sliced mushrooms and the seasons.
3. Simmer for about 20 minutes on medium heat.
4. Place about two dippers of the sauce in the bottom of a large microwave casserole dish. Add about 3 noodles. Add about ½ mozzarella and sprinkle the Parmesan cheese, and the Romano cheese too.
5. Keep on layering the sauce, the cheeses and the noodles, until everything is used up. Finishing with the 3 cheeses on top. Let set up about 1 hour.
6. Bake in a microwave once for 30 minutes on 8 power or until noodles are done.

*Let set up about 20 minutes before serving*     *Serves about 8*

# Salisbury Steak

**Ingredients:**
1 pound lean beef
1 ½ teaspoon salt
Pinch of black pepper
½ small onion chopped
1 egg beaten
Seasoned bread crumbs
¼ teaspoon garlic powder

**Directions:**
1. Combine all the above ingredients shape into patties about ¼" think and flatten out.
2. Place in heavy skillet.
3. Cook on each side until medium brown.
4. Place in large Dutch oven.
5. Pour the mushroom sauce over the patties and cook until done, about 40 minutes low heat.

**Mushroom Sauce Ingredients:**
8 ounces fresh sliced mushrooms
½ cup cooking oil
Water
Salt and pepper to taste

**Mushroom Sauce Directions:**
1. Make a roux (brown the flour in hot oil) add the chopped onions cook for 5 to 8 minutes, until nice and brown.
2. Add the mushrooms cook for about 5 to 6 minutes.
3. Add water a little at a time. Stir often.
4. Make enough gravy to cover the meat patties
5. Cook on medium beat about 30 minutes be careful not to allow the meat patties to stick.
6. Add more water a little at a time.

*Serve hot with rice or mashed potacloves.*
*Serves 6*

# Spaghetti, Meat, and Cheese Casserole Mamma II

### Ingredients:
1 ½ pound ground beef
1 32 ounce jar Ragu spaghetti sauce
½ medium onion chopped fine
3 cloves garlic chopped fine
2 Tablespoons parsley chopped
4 green onions chopped
1 bell pepper chopped
1 ½ pounds cheddar cheese grated
1 pound spaghetti

### Directions:
1. Brown the ground beef and drain well, remove as much oil as possible.
2. Add the spaghetti sauce and all the vegetables, cook over medium heat about 25 to 30 minutes until tender, stirring often.
3. Cook the spaghetti until tender about 10 minutes or follow the directions on the package
4. Mix the spaghetti into the meat mixture stir well
5. Make 3 layers of spaghetti and meat mixture then a layer of grated cheese, ending with cheese on top.
6. Bake in preheated oven 350° F for 20 minutes (just to melt the cheese, turn the pan around and bake for another 10 minutes until lightly brown.

*Serves 7 to 8*

# Stuffed Green Peppers

**Ingredients:**
4 green peppers
1 pound ground beef
2/3 cups Italian bread crumbs
1 egg well beaten
¼ cup chopped bell pepper (use tops from peppers)
1 Tablespoon parsley
1 small onion chopped
4 green onions (Shallots-both tops and bottoms)
4 Tablespoons butter
2 or 3 cloves garlic chopped
Salt and pepper and cayenne pepper to taste

**Directions:**
1. Cut the tops off the peppers, chop them up should be about ¼ cup set aside.
2. Place the whole pepper into cold water, bring to a boil, boil about 5 minutes. Remove from the water and save them.
3. Melt the butter in a medium size sauce pan, add the onions, green onions, garlic, and the chopped bell pepper tops.
4. Add the salt pepper, set aside.
5. In a large sauce pan cook the ground beef drain off all the fat. Add the onion mixture to the meat mixture, stir well to mix.
6. Add the beaten egg and the bread crumbs.
7. Taste to see if more salt or pepper is need, if so adjust to seasonings at this time.
8. Stuff into the pre-boiled green peppers.
9. Sprinkle a little bread crumbs over the tops add cubs of butter on each top.

*Serves 4*

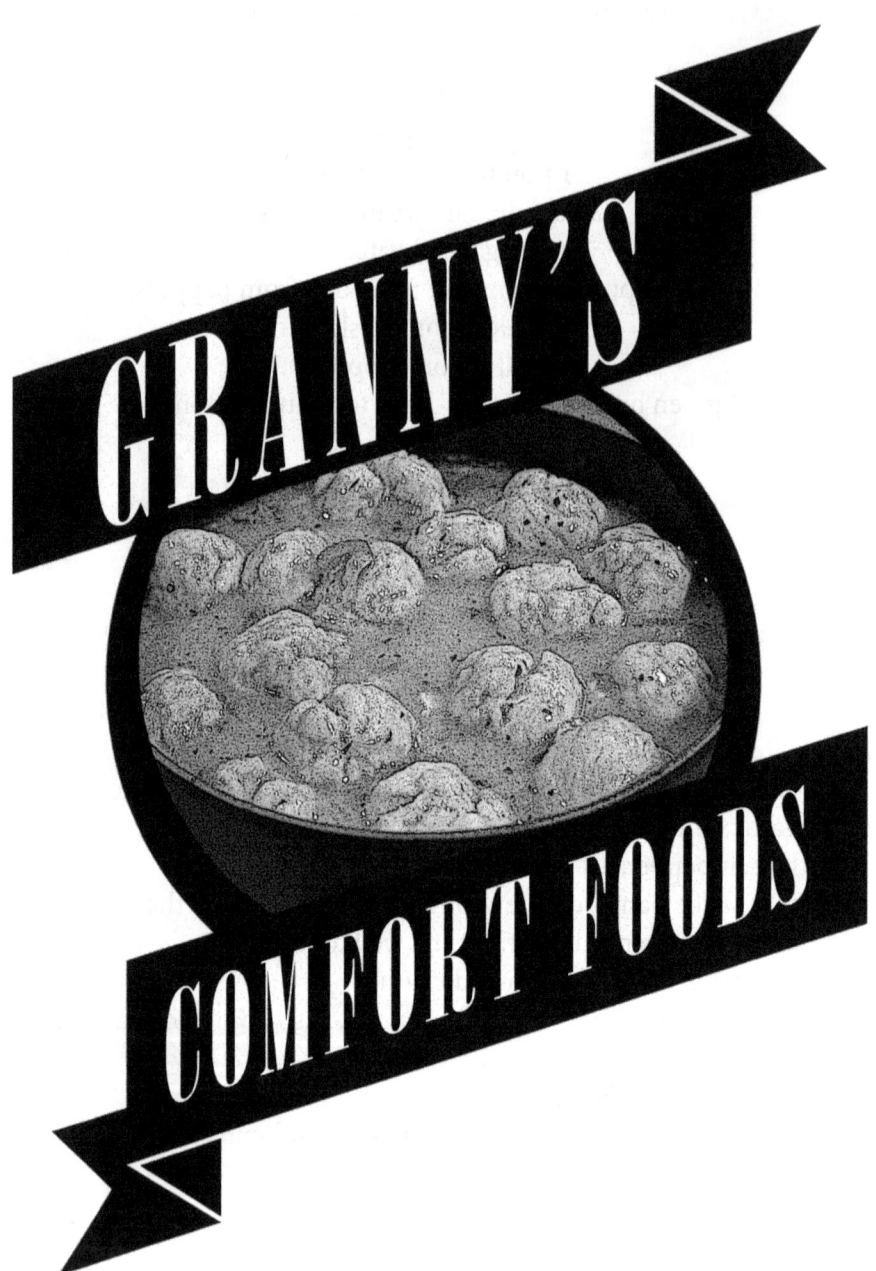

# Chicken and Dumplings

**Ingredients:**
1 cup of roux mix and gravy mix
2 large onions chopped
3 cloves garlic chopped
1 bell pepper chopped
½ cup green onions (tops and bottoms)
Water
Creole seasonings or salt and pepper to taste

**Directions:**
1. Wash and skin the whole chicken Place the "bird" in a large pot cover with water.
2. Place 1 chopped onion in the stock pot with the water and the chicken.
3. Boil until the chicken is tender.
4. Remove the chicken and let it cool.
5. De bone and remove all the meat off the bones, place back into the stock pot.
6. Add the green onions, parsley, garlic, bell pepper, and the remaining 1 onion.
7. Add the roux mix to the cold water, make a think paste.
8. Stir, well and cook just until the vegetables are tender, about 20 to 390 minutes.

**Dumplings Ingredients:**
3 cups Biscuit mix
1 cup milk

Drop in the dumplings. Mix together and drop into hot chicken and gray cover and simmer for about 10 minutes.

*Serves 8 to 10*

# Chicken Sauce Piquante

**Ingredients:**
5 to 6 pounds stewing hen
½ cups cooking oil
½ cups flour
2 ½ cups chopped celery
1 cup green pepper chopped
2 large cans tomato sauce or 1 6 ounce can of tomato paste
3 to 4 cups hot water
3 to 4 cloves garlic
2 to 3 bay leaves
½ cup green onion chopped
¼ cup chopped parsley
Salt and pepper to taste
1/8 teaspoon thyme

**Directions:**
1. Cut the chicken into serving pieces ( I always skin the bird, and season well.)
2. Brown in hot oil and set aside.
3. Add the flour to the chicken drippings and the oil, fry until the flour is light drown.
4. Add the onions celery, bell pepper, and garlic. Cook for about 10 minutes stirring often.
5. Add the cooked chicken, tomato sauce, hot water and the bay leaves.
6. Cover and cook on low heat simmering until the chicken is tender, about 2 to 2 ½ hours.
7. Add the green onions and parsley and cook 15 to 20 minutes longer (taste to see if more salt is needed).

Serve over hot rice *Serves 8*

# Deep Fried Turkey A LA Tommy

**Ingredients:**
1 10 pound turkey or under
1 gallon + 1 quart cooking oil (peanut oil is the best for this receipt)
1 large plastic bag ( unscented)
A lot of Creole seasoning or salt and pepper.
Large deep fryer, or Cajun cooker.

**Directions:**
1. Season the turkey inside and out with a lot of season, use an injector.
2. Please the seasoned turkey in a plastic bag, then place in the refrigerator for 24 to 48 hours to all the seasonings to "mellow" set.
3. In a large deep fryer or the Cajun cooker place the cooking oil, *Tommy has a homemade cooker. (He uses a stainless steel cold drink can and welded the handles on it for carrying.) He also made a still rod to hold the turkey I think now you can buy the kit.
4. When the oil reaches 350° F, place the turkey in the heated oil be very careful the hot oil can burn very bad. You will need a meat thermometer for cooking the turkey.
5. Cook the turkey about 55 minutes.

# Honey BBQ Chicken

**Ingredients:**
2 fryers chicken skinned and cut up
½ cup orange juice
1 cup BBQ sauce
1/3 cup honey
½ cup cooking oil
½ teaspoon dry sweet basil (crushed)
Salt and pepper to taste

**Directions:**
1. Wash, skin, and cut up the chickens.
2. Place the chicken in a deep pan or a large dish.
3. Combine the remaining ingredients in a covered jar; shake to blend.
4. Pour the sauce over the chicken.
5. Cover the chicken with plastic wrap and place in the refrigerator for 4 hours, turning the chicken over and over again about 6 times.
6. Drain the chicken and throw away the sauce.
7. Place the chicken on the hot grill.
8. Baste with new BBQ sauce, honey and O.J.

*Serve 6 to 8*

# Italian Chicken Spaghetti Casserole

**Ingredients:**
1 chicken 3 to 4 pounds
3 cups water
1 chopped onion
½ cup green onions chopped
1 teaspoon fresh chopped parsley
2 cans Italian stew tomacloves (well seasoned)
1 4 ounce can sliced mushroom
1 can tomato paste
2 teaspoon salt (add a little at a time to you get the taste to your liking, you can always add more but you can never take out)
¼ teaspoon cayenne pepper
¼ garlic powder or 2 cloves of fresh garlic chopped fine
¼ teaspoon sweet basil crushed
1 ½ cups boiling water
1 pound spaghetti

**Directions:**
1. Skin the chicken and place in a large pot. Boil until tender. Add the chopped onions, green onions, parsley, and garlic, cook until the chicken is tender.
2. Remove the chicken from the pot, place on platter allow to cool.
3. De bone the chicken and cut into chunks.
4. Measure the water or stock that the chicken was cooked in adding if needed.
5. Place tomacloves, mushrooms, tomato paste, salt and pepper garlic powder not both.
6. Simmer for about 50 minutes until everything is well blended and the vegetables are done.
7. Cook the spaghetti according to the directions.

*Serves 6 to 8*

# Alligator Sauce Piquante

**Ingredients:**
4 pounds alligator meat
1 pound smoked sausage
½ cup cooking oil
½ cup flour
2 ½ cups chopped onions
1 cup chopped celery
4 cloves garlic
4 cups hot water
3 bay leaves
½ cup green onions (tops and bottoms)
¼ cup parsley chopped
3 cans "retell" tomacloves
1 can tomato paste
8 ounce fresh mushrooms sliced
1 Tablespoon sugar
½ teaspoon nutmeg

**Directions:**
1. Heat the cooking oil and alligator until lightly brown, remove and set aside.
2. Make a roux with the oil by adding flour, cook until nice and dark brown.
3. Add the onions, garlic, celery, and green onions. Cook until the vegetable are tender about 10 minutes.
4. Add hot water, stir and cook about 10 minutes.
5. Add the tomacloves and the tomato paste.
6. Place water into the tomato paste can and rinse out. A total of 3 cans of water.
7. Mix well, add the smoked sausage and the browned alligator.
8. Simmer about 2 hours add the fresh mushrooms slices, sugar, and the nutmeg stir well.
9. Add more hot water if needed.
10. Cook about 30 minutes more until the alligator meat is tender.

Serve over Hot rice
*Serves about 10 to 12*

# Beef Jerky

**Ingredients:**
3 Tablespoons garlic powder
3 Tablespoons onion powder
10 ounces soy sauce
3 Tablespoons Creole seasoning
2 packages meat marinade powder
3 pounds meat (beef or deer)
1 bottle Worcestershire sauce
4 to 6 ounces of liquid smoke

**Directions:**
1. Remove all traces of fat from meat, cut into long strips.
2. Mix together all the above ingredients and chill.
3. Be sure to completely cover the meat with the mixture.
4. Marinade for 12 to 24 hours, turning the meat often.
5. Lay the marinade strips on a oven rack. Place the rack on a cookie sheet or a shallow pan. (to catch the drippings)
6. Cook in a low oven heat of 150° F for 8 to 10 hours, or until completely dry. They get crisper the longer they bake.
7. Store the cool jerky in air tight zip lock bags.

You can also use a dehydrator. Cook long and slow about 12 to 17 hours. Rotate the racks as the bottoms racks will dry faster. They will last a long time once stores, however, at my house its more or less a day or two.

# Daddy's Irish Stew

**Ingredients:**
2 pounds boneless lamb* cut into 1" cubs
2 teaspoon salt
¼ teaspoon pepper
1 small bay leaf (whole)
2 medium carrots peeled and cut into ½ circles
2 onions slice thin
4 to 6 Irish potacloves
1 can green pees
¼ cup cooking oil
½ cup flour
2 cloves garlic chopped fine
Water

**Directions:**
1. Season the meat* (I use what dad used, lamb) with salt and pepper.
2. Make a strong roux brown the flour in the hot oil. (Make it rather dark, be careful not to burn the flour.)
3. Add the onions and cook until they are tender about 10 minutes or a little more.
4. Add the meat, and the seasonings cook the meat until brown on both sides turning the meat regular so it does not burn.
5. Add water, carrots, and the potacloves.
6. The gray should not be to thick or to thin, add more water if needed, add corn starch if it to thin.
7. Taste the gray, add more seasoning if needed.
8. When almost done add the can of peas liquid and all.
9. Cook on low heat for another 8 to 10 minutes.

Serve the stew with hot rice, home made bread, biscuits or home made noodles.

*Serves 6 to 8*

# Hasenpfeffer Rabbit Stew

**Ingredients:**
1 4 to 4 ½ pound rabbit
½ cup white vinegar
1 ½ cup water
1 cup red wine 1 medium onion sliced
6 to 7 whole peppers corns red or black
¾ teaspoon whole cloves
1 teaspoon allspice
¾ teaspoon garlic powder or 6 cloves chopped fresh garlic
1 bay leaf crushed
Salt and pepper to taste
4 Tablespoons flour
4 Tablespoon oil

**Directions:**
1. Clean and cut the rabbit into surviving size pieces (set aside)
2. Make a marinade with the vinegar, water, wine, onion pepper corns, cloves, allspice, garlic powder and crushed bay leaf.
3. Bring to boil take off heat and set aside to cool.
4. When the vinegar marinade is cool place the rabbit into the mixture.
5. Cover and place into the refrigerator for 36 to 48 hours, turning several times each day.
6. Drain the rabbit and save the liquid.
7. Dry off the rabbit rib the rabbit with salt and pepper, season well.
8. Place flour in a deep dish and roll the seasoned rabbit into the flour, until well coated add more flour if needed.
9. In a heavy dutch oven heat the oil or the butter using medium heat.
10 Add the floured rabbit to the hot oil cook until well brown turning over often.
11. Strain the vinegar marinade, and use only the liquid part, add it to the rabbit.
12. Cover and simmer well stirring every now and then.
13. Cook about 50 minutes taste the liquid to see if more salt and pepper is needed.
14. Thicken the juices with a mixture of 2 Tablespoons of corn starch and ¼ cup of cold water. Add to the rabbit mixture.

*Serves 4 to 6*

# Old Fashion Italian Meat balls and Spaghetti

**Meat Ball Ingredients:**
½ pound ground beef
½ pound ground veal
6 cloves garlic chopped very fine
½ teaspoon chopped parsley
½ teaspoon sweet basil crushed
3 teaspoon grated Parmesan cheese
Salt and pepper to taste
½ teaspoon thyme crushed
2 eggs beaten
½ cup water
1 cup Italian seasoned dry bread crumbs

**Directions:**
1. Mix all together, make into ball (large ones or small ones)
2. Brown in oil or in the oven, before adding sauce.


**Sauce Ingredients:**
1 medium onion chopped very fine
2 cans "Contadina" Italian tomato paste
6 cans of water
2 teaspoons sugar
½ teaspoon thyme crushed
2 cloves garlic
½ teaspoon sweet basil (crushed)
3 bay leaves (Leave whole, and remove after the sauce is finished cooking)
Season with salt and pepper as needed.

**Directions:**
1. Make the meat balls and set aside until the sauce is finished.
2. Fry the onions until they are very soft about 15 minutes.
3. Add the tomato paste, rinse the cans out with water and place into the

pot with the onions and the tomato paste.

4. Add the rest of the sauce ingredients to the pot, let simmer about 3 hours before adding meat balls that browned, stir well adding more water if necessary.

5. Now add the meat balls (that we browned) and cook about 1 hour longer, keep adding water whenever it becomes necessary.

Cooking the spaghetti according to the package directions.

*Serves 4 to 6*

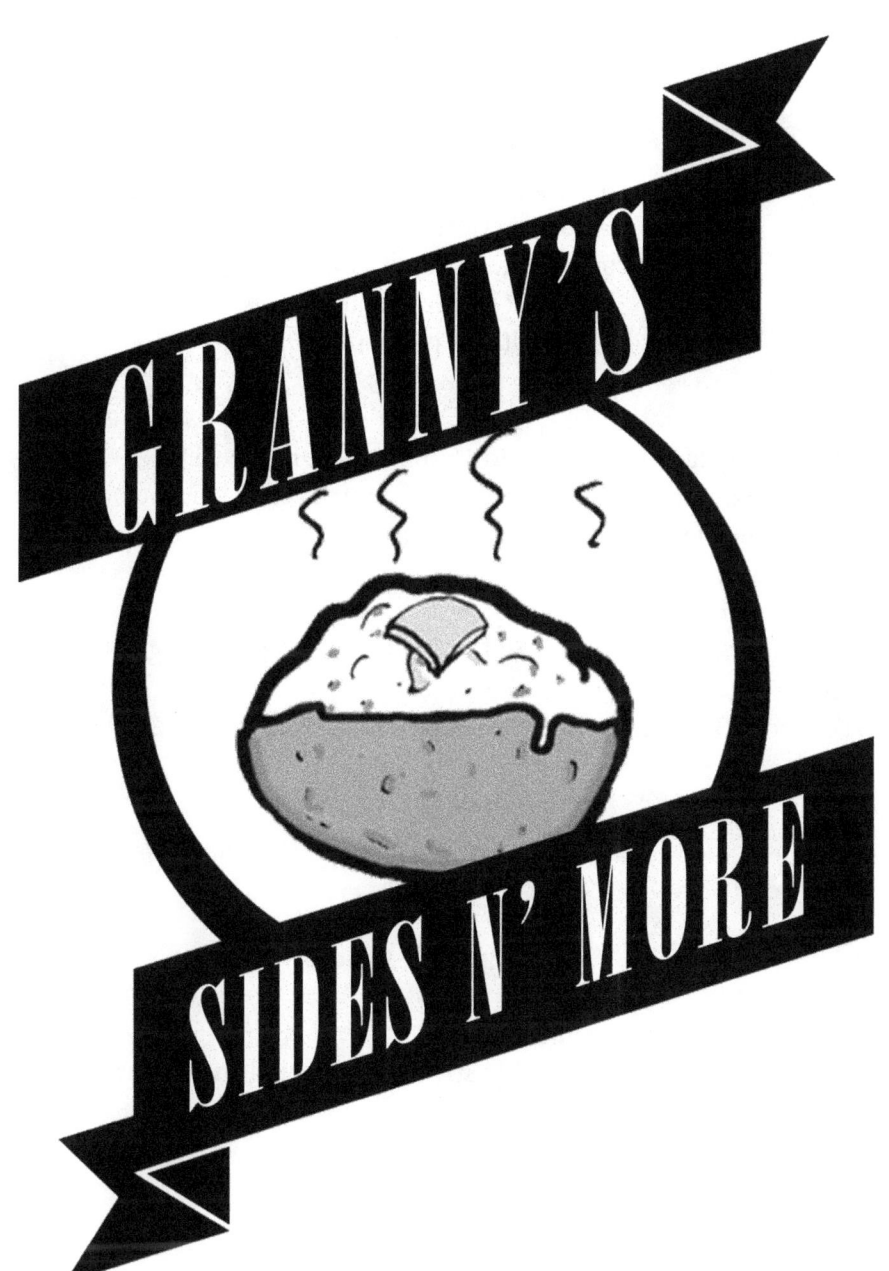

# Cabbage Casserole

**Ingredients:**
1 medium head cabbage (cut up)
1 medium onion chopped
1 cup grated American or Cheddar cheese
*2 cups medium think white sauce
½ stick butter (melted)
Salt and pepper

**Directions:**
1. Boil the cabbage for about 10 to 15 minutes. Drain well.
2. Brown the onions in the melted butter, pour over the drained cabbage.
3. Pour a layer of whit sauce in a casserole dish.
4 . Now place a layer of cabbage.
5. Sprinkle some grated cheese.
6. Continue the layering until all the food is used up. Ending with a layer of cheese.
7. Bake about 30 minutes in a preheated oven 325° F.

**\*White sauce Ingredients:**
2 tablespoons corn starch
2 cups milk
4 Tablespoons butter
Salt and pepper to taste

**Directions:**
1. In a saucepan melt the butter.
2. Mix the corn starch in the milk, stir well, so there is no lumps.
3. Add the milk to the melted butter.
4. Bring to boil, cook about 1 to 2 minutes.

*Makes 2 cups*

# Corn Fritters

**Ingredients:**
2 eggs slightly beaten
½ cup milk
2 Tablespoons cooking oil
1 ½ cups sifted flour
2 teaspoons baking powder
1 teaspoon salt
1 ½ cups corn

**Directions:**
1. Combine the beaten eggs, oil, and the milk.
2. Add the dry ingredients all at once, Mixing only until the flour is damp.
3. Add the corn.
4. Drop into the hot oil (about 350° F to 365° F).
5 Fry until golden brown about 4 to 5 minutes.

*Makes 2 dozen*

# Corn Relish A La Refrigerator Method

**Ingredients:**
6 ears fresh corn
½ green pepper chopped
½ red pepper ( not hot) chopped
5 stems celery chopped
1 large onion chopped
1 toe garlic chopped
2/3 cups salad oil
3 tablespoons wine vinegar
2 teaspoons salt
1 teaspoon black pepper
1 ¼ teaspoons dry mustard

**Directions:**
1. Cook the corn in water about 6 to 10 minutes.
2. Cool the corn, and cut off the cobs.
3. Add the remaining ingredients.
4. Chill several hours before serving.
5. Keep refrigerated.

Excellent with BBQ foods

# Corn with Basil

**Ingredients:**
2 cans corn or 2 packages frozen corn or 6 fresh corn
1 medium onion chopped
1 stem celery chopped fine
4 Tablespoons butter or oleo
1 red bell pepper (not hot)
½ teaspoon dry sweet basil powder
½ teaspoon chopped parsley
6 green onions chopped
Salt and pepper to taste

**Directions:**
1. If using fresh corn cook for 10 minutes in boiling water, when cool cut off the cob.
2. If using frozen corn defrost in the microwave for about 5 minutes on the defrost cycle. If using can corn drain well.
3. Cook the onions, celery, green onions, parsley, red sweet bell pepper, and the corn in the butter. Cook until the onions are tender. (about 10 minutes) stir often.
4. Stir in the rest of the ingredients, then turn to low and cover.
5. Cook about 5 to 6 minutes, stir well.

*Serves 4 to 6*

# Cream of Turnips

**Ingredients:**
6 turnips roots (white an purple)
3 Tablespoons butter
2 tablespoons flour
1 ½ cups milk
1 ½ Tablespoon sugar
Salt to taste

**Directions:**
1. Peel and slice the turnips ½" circles.
2. Boil just until tender, drain well.
3. Make a medium white sauce, by melting the butter, adding the flour a little at a time, now add the milk slowly. Stir well.
4. Stir in the salt and sugar and add the turnips.

*Serves 3 to 4*

# Eggplant Fritters A La Grandma Huber

**Ingredients:**
1 medium size eggplant
3 Tablespoons sugar
¼ teaspoon nutmeg
1 egg well beaten
4 to 5 tablespoons flour (depends on the size eggplant)
2 ½ teaspoon baking powder
Powder sugar

**Directions:**
1. Wash and peel the eggplant, cut into 1" pieces and boil until tender.
2. Drain, add sugar, nutmeg, flour, egg, and the baking powder.
3. Let "set up" about 30 minutes.
4. In a skillet, heat oil, place a large spoonful of the mixture into the hot oil.
5. Cook until brown, on both sides, turning only once.
6. Remove from the skillet and sprinkle with powder sugar.
7. Keep hot until all are cooked.

*Serves 8*

# Eggplant Parmesan

**Ingredients:**
2 eggs beaten + 3 Tablespoons water
1 medium eggplant
1 cup Italian bread crumbs
¼ cup cooking oil
1 pound sweet Italian sausage
4 cups tomato sauce
12 ounces grated Mozzarella Cheese
Salt and pepper to taste
Granted Parmesan cheese
Olive oil

**Directions:**
1. Wash and peel the eggplant, cut into think slices.
2. Dip the eggplant slices into the egg and water mixture.
3. The sprinkle the salt and pepper on each slice, then into the bread crumbs.
4. Heat the cooking oil in a large skillet, fry the eggplant (a few slices at a time) until golden brown.
5. Drain on paper towel.
6. Spread a little tomato sauce on the bottom of the baking dish. Place the cooked eggplant on top of the sauce. Now place the cooked sausage on top the eggplant. Add some cheese.
7. More another layer.
8. End with tomato sauce.
9. Bake about 350° F for about 30 minutes.

*Serves 6*

# Fried Green Tomatoes

**Ingredients:**
Shortening
2 green tomatoes
1 egg + 2 tablespoons water
Italian bread crumbs
Salt and pepper

**Directions:**
1. Heat the oil in a heavy skillet.
2. Slice the tomatoes into ¼" circles.
3. Beat the eggs and add the water.
4. Dip the tomatoes slices into the egg mixture.
5. Sprinkle the salt and pepper on each slice.
6. Now dip to tomato slice into the brad crumbs.
7. Fry in the hot shortening.
8. Serve hot.

*Serves 3 to 4*

# Fried Okra

**Ingredients:**
1 to ½ pound okra sliced
2 eggs well beaten + 2 Tablespoons water
Salt and pepper to taste
Seasoned bread crumbs or yellow corn meal

**Directions:**
1. Wash and drain the okra, cut the okra into ¼" circles.
2. Place some okra into the egg mixture.
3. With a slotted spoon remove the okra and place the okra into the dry bread crumbs, sprinkle with salt and pepper.
4. With a fork "stir up" the okra into the bread crumbs.
5. Place into the hot oil, cook until well browned.
6. Place on paper towel to drain, keep hot until all the okra is cooked.

*Serves 6*

# Grandma Becker's German Potato Pancakes (Kartoffelnuffer)

**Ingredients:**
4 large white potatoes
1 small onion
1 egg beaten well
3 Tablespoons flour
1 teaspoon salt
¼ teaspoon black pepper
2 pinches garlic powder
Vegetable oil

**Directions:**
1. Using a hand grater, shred the potatoes, make about 2 ½ cups.
2. Squeeze the potatoes to remove liquid, save the liquid in a small bowl.
3. Grate the onions, place them with the egg, salt, flour, pepper, and garlic powder in a bowl.
4. Discard the top portion of the potato liquid, use the bottom part; it has the most starch. (About 1/8 cup) Stir this liquid into the potato mixture.
5. Heat oven 350° F.
6. In a large heavy skillet heat the oil and cook the pancakes. Cook about 3 minutes on each side, they should be brown and crispy on each side.
7. Drain on paper towels, keep hot in the oven until ready to serve.

*Serve 4 to 6*

# Mexican Corn Casserole

**Ingredients:**
1 teaspoon garlic powder
2 cans yellow corn, seasoned with red and green bell peppers.
2 cans cream yellow corn
1 can seasoned stewed sliced tomatoes
1 stick butter or oleo
¼ cup grated American or Cheddar cheese
1 large onion chopped

**Directions:**
1. Place the butter and the onions in a heavy skillet, saute for 5 minutes.
2. Add all the corn and the tomatoes.
3. Add the garlic powder salt, pepper, stir well, and often.
4. Butter a casserole dish, place the corn mixture into the dish.
5. Sprinkle the cheese on top the corn mixture.
6. Bake in preheated oven 350° F cook about 8 minutes, until cheese is melted and bubbly.

*Serves 6*

# Red Cabbage and Apples

**Ingredients:**
3 tablespoons butter or oleo
1 large onion chopped fine
1 medium cabbage about 1 ½ to 2 pounds
3 red apples (Rome or Winesap) peeled, cored and sliced
¾ cups water
½ cup red wine
3 tablespoons apple cider vinegar
2 teaspoons sugar
1 teaspoon salt
2 pinches of fresh ground black pepper
½ teaspoon nutmeg
1 teaspoon lemon peel

**Directions:**
1, Melt the butter in a large saucepan on medium heat.
2. Add onions and cook 10 minutes or until onions are tender.
3. Add cabbage and apple, cook about 10 minutes stirring 3 times.
4. Add wine, water, vinegar, sugar, nutmeg, and the pepper.
5. Cover and cook over low heat about 25 minutes (until cabbage is tender).
6. If the cabbage is to dry add a little not water.
7. Just before the cabbage is done stir in the lemon peel.
8. Serve hot.

*6 to 8 servings*

# Smothered Potatoes

### Ingredients:
5 pounds Irish potatoes
1 large onion chopped
3 tablespoons cooking oil
Salt and pepper to taste

**Directions:**
1. Peel the potatoes and cut about ¼" think circles, place them into cold water until ready for use.
2. In a large Dutch oven, heat the oil (about 4 minutes).
3. Add the potatoes, (be sure that you dry them off first) cook about 10 minutes or medium heat stir often.
4. Add the chopped onions, stir once again be careful not to break up the potatoes.
5. Add the seasonings, stir often to keep them from sticking.
6. Turn the fire down to low continue to cook until the potatoes are tender.

*Serves about 6 to 8*

# Sweet Potato Casserole

**Ingredients:**
1 large can sweet potatoes
1 small can pineapples tidbits
3 Tablespoons butter or oleo
2 Tablespoons brown sugar
½ teaspoon cinnamon
Little marshmallows

**Directions:**
1. Drain the syrup from the sweet potatoes (save juice)
2. Drain the pineapple (save juice)
3. Add the sugar to the two juices and cook until syrupy
4. Add the sweet potatoes, butter and the cinnamon
5. Beat with electric mixer until fluffy
6. Add the pineapple
7. Place in buttered casserole dish
8. Top with marshmallows and bake in preheated oven 350° F for 25 minutes or until brown.

Serves 6

# Cinnamon Bread

**Ingredients:**
6-7 ½ cups flour
2 packages yeast
2 cups milk
¼ white sugar
¼ cup butter

2 teaspoon 3 eggs

1. Preheat oven to 375° F
2. In a large mixer bowl combine 3 cups flour and the yeast each package of yeast = 2 ¼ teaspoons (if using bread yeast, measure carefully).
3. In a sauce pan, heat the milk sugar, butter and the salt (just until warm about 114° to 120° F and the butter is almost melted.)
4. Stir constantly.
5. Add the flour mixture.
6. Eggs and beat ½ minute on low.
7. Now beat on high 3 minutes scraping the sides of the bowl.
8. Stir in as mush of the remaining flour as you can using a mixing spoon.
9. Roll each half into 15" X 7" rectangle. (May also be made into sweet rolls by cutting each rectangle into ¾")
10. Brush each surface of the dough with melted butter.
11. Mix 2/3 cups sugar with 3 teaspoons cinnamon.
12. Roll up like a jelly roll, seal the ends and turn under. Place in a greased loaf pan. Cover and let rise until double in size (about 35 to 40 minutes.)
13. Bake for 35 to 40 minutes.

**Sugar Icing Ingredients:**
1 cup powder sugar
¼ to ½ teaspoon vanilla (white if possible)
2 Tablespoons milk

**Directions:**
1. Stir together, until it is smooth enough to drizzle.
2. Drizzle warm loaf or over sweet rolls with sugar icing.

# Egg Bread—Sweet Dough

**Ingredients:**
6-7 ½ cups flour
2 packages yeast
2 cups milk
¼ white sugar
¼ cup butter
2 teaspoon
3 eggs

**Directions:**
1. Preheat oven to 375 F.
2. In a large mixer bowl combine 3 cups flour and the yeast each package of yeast = 2 ¼ teaspoons (if using bread yeast, measure carefully)
3. In a sauce pan, heat the milk sugar, butter and the salt (until warm about 114° to 120° F and the butter is almost melted.)
4. Stir constantly. Add the flour mixture.
5 Eggs and beat ½ minute on low.
6. Now beat on high 3 minutes scraping the sides of the bowl.
7. Stir in as mush of the remaining flour as you can using a mixing spoon.
8. Turnout on a floured table or large working counter.
9. Knead in enough flour to make a stiff dough that is smooth, about 6 to 7 minutes.
10. Place in a large bowl that has been greased.
11. Cover ( I use a sheet of waxed paper) and let it raise until double in size. (about 1 ½ hours).
12. Punch down, and divide into half.
13. Shape into 2 loaves, place into 2 pans. Cover and let rise until double in size (about 35 to 40 minutes.)
14. Bake 35 to 40 minutes.

# Whole Wheat Batter Bread

**Ingredients:**
1 package dry yeast
1 ¼ cup warm water
2 tablespoons honey
2 teaspoon salt
2 Tablespoon butter
1 cup whole wheat flour
2 cups white flour
1 tablespoons baking powder.

**Directions:**
1. Preheat oven to 375° F.
2. In a mixing blow dissolve the yeast in the warm water. Add butter and half of the flour.
3. Beat with electric mixer for 2 minutes.
4. With a spoon, blend in the rest of the flour until the batter is formed (about 1 ½ minutes).
5. Cover and let rise until double the size about 30 minutes.
6. Stir down batter beat about 25 minutes.
7. Spread the batter evenly into buttered pan, smooth out the top of the loft.
8. Let rise about 40 minutes.
9. Bake for 40 to 45 minutes.

*Makes 1 loaf*

# Fresh Strawberry Bread

**Ingredients:**
2 cups flour
1 teaspoon salt
2 teaspoon grated lemon peel
½ teaspoon nutmeg
2 eggs beaten
½ cup honey
1 ½ cup fresh strawberries sliced
¾ cup chopped pecans
¼ cup cooking oil

**Directions:**
1. Preheat oven to 350° F.
2. Stir together all the dry ingredients.
3. Combine the eggs, honey and oil, stir in the sliced strawberries and the pecans.
4. Add the liquid ingredients to the dry, stirring just to the flour is moist.
5. Butter 1 loaf pans, pour in the mixture.
6. Bake in a for 50-55 minutes.
7. Cool for 15 minutes before removing from the pan.
8. Place on a wire baking rack to finish cooling.

*Makes 2 loaves*

# Pineapple Pecan Bread

**Ingredients:**
1 stick butter or oleo
½ cup of sugar
2 eggs beaten
1 ¾ cups flour
½ teaspoon baking powder
¼ teaspoon soda
¼ teaspoon salt
½ cup butter milk
1 cup drained crushed pineapple
1/3 cup chopped pecans

**Directions:**
1. Preheat oven to 350° F.
2. Grease 9"x 5" loaf pan.
3. In a large bowl, beat the butter and the sugar until light and fluffy.
4. Add the egg, 1 at a time, beat well after each addition.
5. Add flour, baking powder, backing soda, salt, and milk.
6. Beat well and add the lemon peel and beat again.
7. Slowly stir in the well drained pineapple and pecans.
8. Pout into the prepared pan.
9. Bake on 350° F 45- 50 minutes or until toothpick comes out clean, when placed in the center.
10. Cool 10 minutes before removing from the pan, place onto wire cake rack.
11. Serve with honey butter. (1 stick of butter or oleo, and 2 to 3 ounces of honey; mix well with an electric mixer.)

*Makes 1 loaf*

# No Bake "Welfare" Cookies

**Ingredients:**
½ cup milk
2 cups sugar
½ cup oleo
3 Tablespoons cocoa
1 Tablespoons vanilla
3 cups raw oatmeal (Quick cook)
1 cup peanut butter (plan or crunchy)
1 cup chopped pecans
1 cup raisons or 1 cup coconut flakes

**Directions:**
1. Mix the milk, sugar, oleo, and the cocoa in a glass measuring cup.
2. Cook in the microwave oven about 3 minutes until it comes to a boil.
3. Add the vanilla, oatmeal and peanut butter.
4. Add either the pecans, raisons or the coconut flakes.
5. Use a Tablespoon and drop onto wax paper, let air dry.

I names these cookies "Welfare Cookies" because one of my friends had foster children. She would give me the USDA oatmeal and peanut butter to make the cookies. The children really enjoyed them, and so did my kids. They are really easy to make and the children can help.

*Makes about 5 dozen*

# Quickie Butterscotch Fudge

**Ingredients:**
1 2/3 cups white sugar
2/3 cup (1 small pet milk)
Pinch of salt
1 6 ounces butterscotch bits
½ cup tiny marshmallows
1 cup pecans broken
1 Tablespoon butterscotch or vanilla flavoring

**Directions:**
1. Cover a baking dish 9"x 5" with tin foil, then butter the foil.
2. Preheat over to 300° F. Spread the broken pecans on a cookie sheet, place in over.
3. Turn off the over and let the nuts stay in the oven for about 20 minutes. (This will make them crispy).
4. In a 3 quart heavy saucepan, place the sugar, pet milk, and the salt.
5. Cook and stir until sugar dissolves.
6. When the sugar mixture comes to a boil; set a timer and allow to cook for 5 minutes.
7. Remove from heat; add butterscotch candy and the marshmallows. Stir until well blended.
8. Add flavoring and the pecans, beat until thick, about 6 to 8 minutes.
9. Pour into butter dish.
10. Allow to cool and "firm up" before cutting about 2 to 3 hours.

# Red Velvet Cake

**Ingredients:**
½ cup shortening
2 eggs
1 teaspoon vanilla
1 teaspoon baking soda
1 cup buttermilk
1 ½ cup sugar
2 teaspoons cocoa
1 teaspoon salt
2 ½ cups flour
1 tablespoon white vinegar
¼ cup red food color (liquid).

**Directions:**
1. Preheat oven to 350° F.
2. Cream shortening and sugar until fluffy add eggs, one at a time. Beat 1 minute after each addition.
3. Mix cocoa and the food coloring. (make a paste-like-consistency).
4. Add salt.
5. Mix the butter milk with the vanilla.
6. Slowly add the sugar mixture with the flour.
7. Combine the soda and the vinegar, stir into the batter. DO NOT BEAT—ONLY STIR SLIGHTLY.
8. Pour into a greased pan 9"x 13"
9. Bake for about 30 minutes or until done. (When a tooth pick comes out clean when placed in the center of the cake.)
10. Cool and frost with your favorite frosting.

# Rice Pudding

**Ingredients:**
2 cups regular rice (not instant)
2 cups milk
1 ½ cups sugar
1 teaspoon vanilla
1 tablespoon corn starch
1 ½ cups raisons
3 teaspoons ground cinnamon (add more for more taste)

**Directions:**
1. Preheat oven to 275° F.
2. Beat the yoke of the eggs well, add sugar, beat until creamy. Add the milk slowly.
3. Add the cooked rice (left over rice may be used) raisons and the vanilla, stir well.
4. Add the corn starch with a little water (Make a paste), stir this into the rice mixture.
5. Cook on top of the stove or in the microwave for a little while until the mixture is thick.
6. Remove from heat.
7. Beat the rice mixture in a baking dish that has been buttered.
8. Place the rice mixture in a baking dish that has been buttered.
9. Spread the egg whites and sugar mixture over the rice pudding.
10. Bake for 15 minutes, (Just until the topping is golden brown)

*Serves about 6 to 8*

# Sugar Anise Cookies

**Ingredients:**
½ cup butter or oleo
¼ cup Crisco shortening
1 ¼ cup Sifted powdered sugar
1 egg beaten
1 teaspoon oil anise
2 cups flour
1 teaspoon baking powder
½ teaspoon salt
¼ teaspoon baking soda

**Directions:**
1. Preheat over to 375° F.
2. Cream butter, shortening and sugar, beat well until fluffy.
3. Add egg and the flavoring.
4. Add the shifted flour, the baking powder, salt and baking soda. Stir into the creamed mixture.
5. Shape into 2 rolls 6 ½ inches long.
6. Wrap in wax paper, or plastic wrap.
7. Chill well.
8. Cut in ¼ inch slices and place on a cookie sheet that is NOT GREASED.
9. Press a half pecan on each slice.
10. Bake 8 to 10 minutes.

*Makes 3 to 4 dozen*

# Sugared Pecans

### Ingredients:
1 ½ cups sugar
½ cup water
¼ cup honey
½ teaspoon maple or vanilla flavoring
3 cups pecan halves

### Directions:
1. Bring the sugar, water, and the honey to a boil.
2. Low the heat and continue to cook until the soft ball stage is at 238° F
3. Remove from heat, add pecans, and the flavoring
4. Stir carefully (remember it is very hot and you can get burned)
5. Add the flavoring, and continue to stir until very creamy.
6. Drop onto wax paper, separate before it gets to hard.

# Sweet Potato Pie

### Ingredients:
6 Fresh sweet potatoes
2 cups white sugar
2 sticks butter
2 teaspoons vanilla
2 ½ Tablespoons flour ( sprinkled into the mixture to thicken)

### Directions:
1. Cook the potatoes in the microwave on high for 10 minutes, until done.
2. Peel and mash once cooled.
3. Whip the butter and the sugar, add the mashed yams and vanilla. Sprinkle the flour over this mixture and stir well.
4. Place into 2 frozen pie shells.

*Makes 2 pies*

# Anise Tea Cakes

### Ingredients:
1 cup Crisco shortening
1 cup sugar
2 eggs well beaten
2 teaspoons anise seeds
1 cup sour cream
5 cups flour
2 heaping teaspoons baking powder
2 to 4 drops anise oil
1 ¼ teaspoon salt
1 teaspoon baking soda

### Directions:
1. Cream shortening, sugar, and eggs. Add flour, salt, baking powder and the baking soda.
2. Add the anise oil and the anise seeds, add the sour cream. Mix well.
3. Chill for 2 hours.
4. Rollout ¼" thick, cut with a biscuit cutter.
5. Bake in a Preheated oven 375° F for 15 minutes, or until lightly brown.
6. When cool glaze.

### Glaze Ingredients:
1 ½ cups powder sugar
7 Tablespoons milk
1 Tablespoon vanilla

### Directions:
1. Mix together, should be rather thin not like frosting.
2. Spread on cool cookies. Add more sugar if to thin, add more milk if to thick.

*Makes 7 dozen cookies*

# Apple Turnovers

### Ingredients:
2 ½ cups canned apple slices
¾ cups light brown sugar
1 teaspoon cinnamon
½ teaspoon nutmeg
¼ allspice
¼ cup seedless raisins
2 cups flour
2 Tablespoon sugar
½ teaspoon salt
¾ cup shortening
¼ cup water (about)

### Directions:
1. Preheat oven to 425° F unless you are going to fry them*.
2. Drain and chop the apples.
3. Combine the apples with the brown sugar and the spices.
4. Add 1 Tablespoon flour and sugar (this is the filling).
5. Dough: Sift together the flour, the sugar, and salt.
6. "Cut in" the shortening, add enough water to make a firm dough.
7. Roll the dough 1/8 inch thick, cut into squares.
8. Place a small amount of the apple filling in the center of each square.
9. Wet the edges of the pastry with a little water, and fold over. Press firmly together with a dinner folk.
10. Pierce the top of each turnover.
11. Bake for 25 minutes or *deep fry 350° F for 4 to 5 minutes.

If you are in a hurry, just buy the pie dough found in the dairy case, it will look just as good.

# Baked Apples A La Microwave

**Ingredients:**
6 large apples (Rome or Winesap)
¼ cup sugar
4 Tablespoon cinnamon
6 teaspoons butter
Water

**Directions:**
1. Wash the apples wipe dry.
2. Core but do not peel the apples.
3. Pierce the apples with a fork about 3 to 4 times.
4. Place in a glass dish.
5. Mix the sugar and the cinnamon together, divide this mixture between the 6 apples. (Placing the mixture in the center hole of each apple).
6. Place the butter on top of each apple.
7. Add a little water to the dish; (be careful not to disturb the sugar and the butter).
8. Place in the microwave and cook 10 to 12 minutes on 7 power.

*Serves 6*

# Bible Cake

**Ingredients:**
1 cup Judges 5:25 Last cause (butter)
2 cups Jeremiah 6:20 (cane-sugar)
2 teaspoons I Samuel 14:25 Last clause (honey)
6 Jeremiah 17:11 (eggs)
½ cup Judges 4:19 (milk)
2 teaspoons Amos 4:5 (baking powder)
1 cup I Samuel 30:12 second Phase (raisons)
1 cup Nahum 3:12 (chopped figs)
II Chronicles 9:9 to taste (spices - apple pie spice)
I cup Song of Solomon 6:11 (chopped nuts)
4 ½ cups Judges 15:1 (flour)
¼ teaspoon Matthew 5:13 (salt)

**Directions:**
1 Preheat oven to 350° F
2. Cream sugar and butter.
3. Add the eggs one at a time, beating after each addition.
4. Dredge the figs and the nuts in some of the flour. Add alternately with the wet ingredients.
5. Place in a tube pan, and bake for 1 hour or until done.

# BROWNIES

### Ingredients:
1 teaspoon vanilla
1 cake mix (regular size)
1 egg
¼ cup water
½ cup chopped pecan
13" x 9" buttered pan

### Directions:
1. Preheat oven to 350°F.
2. In a medium bowl place the butter egg, water and the vanilla, mix well.
3. Add cake mix and pecans, and stir with spoon.
4. Pour into a buttered pan.
5. Bake for about 25 minutes.

### Frosting Ingredients:
½ cup butter or oleo
¼ cup cocoa
¼ cup pet milk
¼ teaspoon salt
4 cups powdered sugar
¼ cup pecans

### Directions:
1. In a medium saucepan place the cocoa, butter, milk ad the salt. Cook until smooth.
2. Remove from heart stir in the vanilla. Add the sugar, and stir until smooth and creamy.
3. Spread over the hot brownies.
4. Sprinkle the pecans over the frosting.

# Butter Milk Pralines

**Ingredients:**
1 cup butter milk
1 teaspoon baking soda
3 cups white sugar

**Directions:**
1. Cook these 3 ingredients together. Cook to the soft ball stage. When a ball forms in the bottom of a cup of cold water—138°F.
2. Remove from heat, and add 4 cups of pecans (halves if possible), 4 Tablespoons of butter, and 1 teaspoon of vanilla or maple flavor.
3. Beat until creamy.
4. Drop unto wax paper or unto a buttered marble candy slab.

**To make butter milk:**
Add 1 Tablespoon lemon juice or white vinegar into the milk to make 1 cup. (must stand a room temperature for 5 to 20 minutes.

*Makes about 12 to 18 depending on the size you make them*

# Candy Strawberries

**Ingredients:**
1 can condensed milk
2 cups flaked coconut
1 cup ground pecans
2 large boxes of strawberry Jell-O

**Directions:**
1. Combine all the ingredients and mix thoroughly.
2. Chill 1 to 2 hours.
3. Mix ½ cup white sugar with some red food color, mix well.
4. Roll the chilled coconut mixture into small round ball, then shape into berries.
5. Roll in the red sugar mixture or plain strawberry Jell-O .
6. Add plastic green stems for each berry.

# Creole Pralines

**Ingredients:**
4 cups white sugar
¼ cup water
1 ¼ tablespoon butter
1 ¼ teaspoon vinegar
3 cups pecans
1 ¼ maple flavoring (pure)

**Directions:**
1 Place sugar, water, and vinegar in a saucepan and boil to soft boil stage 238° F, add the maple flavoring, butter and the pecans.
2. Continue to cook until syrup when drooped from the end of the spoon spins a thread.
3. Remove from heat and beat 1 minute until grained.
4. With a large spoon scoop out a spoon of the candy place the candy on a butter cookie sheet.

## Daddy's Coconut Pralines

**Ingredients:**
2 cups white sugar
4 cups fresh grated coconut
¾ cup water ( or juice from the coconut)
1 Tablespoon butter (not oleo)

**Directions:**
1. Boil the sugar, water (or juice) and the butter.
2. Cook the mixture until it reaches the soft boil stage 238° F. (Also a soft boil forms in the bottom of a cup of water)
3. Add the fresh coconut, boil slowly until mixture forms a soft boil in a cup of cold water.
4. Mix well, beat until creamy add a few drops of red food coloring. This will make a nice pink color. Great for Christmas.
5. Have platters pre buttered and drop the candy by spoon full.
6. Allow to cool, then lift by running a spatula under each one.
7. When very cold wrap each one in wax paper or in plastic wrap.

## Daddy's Creole Coconut Pie

**Ingredients:**
3 eggs separated
1 cup sugar
1 stick butter
¼ cup milk
1 teaspoon vanilla
3 cups shredded coconut
1 9" unbaked pie shell

**Directions:**
1. Preheat oven to 375° F.
2. Beat whites until stiff and gradually add ¼ cup sugar.
3. Cream butter and remaining sugar, add eggs yokes and blend thoroughly.
4. Add milk and vanilla.
5. Fold the egg whites and the coconut into the butter mixture
6. Pour into pie shell, bake for about 30 minutes.

*Makes 1 pie*

# Daddy's Old Fashioned Sour Cream Cookies

**Ingredients:**
½ cup shortening, butter or oleo
1 cup sugar
1 egg
1 teaspoon vanilla
1 1/3 cups flour
1 teaspoon baking powder
½ teaspoon baking soda
½ teaspoon salt
½ teaspoon nutmeg
½ cup spur cream

**Directions:**
1. Preheat oven 425° F.
2. Mix shortening, sugar, egg, and the vanilla thoroughly.
3. Blend in the dry ingredients.
4. Add the sugar mixture alternately with the sour cream.
5. Divide the dough, roll out to ¼" thick (on a well floured pastry cloth or table).
6. Cut into 2" circles (use biscuit cutter).
7. Place on a greased baking sheet.
8. Sprinkle with sugar.
9. Bake 8 to 10 minutes or until lightly brown.

# Daddy's Pecan Pralines
## (This receipt has been in my family for 125 years)

**Ingredients:**
3 cups sugar (separated)
1 cup pet milk
½ teaspoon baking soda
2 cups pecans (halves if possible)
1 Tablespoon maple flavor

**Directions:**
1 Heat 1 cup sugar until it melts completely (stir constantly, as it will burn fast).
2. Heat 1 cup pet milk to the boiling point.
3. Then add ½ teaspoon baking soda into milk, stir well.
4. Pour the remaining 2 cups sugar, stir well.
5. Cook until the soft ball (138° F or until soft ball forms in a cup of water)
6. Remove from heat and allow to cool. Now add the pecans and the flavoring.
7. Beat until creamy.
8. Drop onto wax paper or buttered slab.

*Makes 12 to 18 depending on the size*

# Easy Dump Cake

**Ingredients:**
1 can crushed pineapple
*1 can cherry pie filling
1 box white cake mix
2 sticks butter or oleo
1 cup chopped pecans

**Directions:**
1. Preheat oven to 350°.
2. Grease a 9" x 13" pan. Dump pineapple and pie filling onto the pan.
3. Mix the cake mix and the butter together
4. Sprinkle over the filling mix.
5. Sprinkle the pecans on top
6. Bake for 30–40 minutes

*Fruit cocktail, blue berry pie filling, lemon pie filling, etc. May be used in place of the cherry pie filling.

# Heavenly Hash Cake

**Ingredients:**
2 sticks butter ( Not oleo)
2 cups white sugar
4 eggs beaten
1 ½ cups flour
1 ½ teaspoon baking powder
¼ cocoa
2 cups chopped pecans
2 teaspoon vanilla
3 cups tiny marshmallows
2/3 cups milk

**Directions:**
1. Preheat oven to 350° F.
2. Cream butter and the eggs, add the sugar.
3. Stir in all the dry (SIFTED) ingredients.
4. Mix well.
5. Add the pecans and the vanilla, and stir again.
6. Place in a greased 13" x 9" x 2" banking pan.
7. Bake in a preheated for 35 to 40 minutes or until done. (When a tooth pick placed into the center of the cake comes out clean).
8. Take out the oven and add tiny marshmallows at once.
9. Wait 5 minutes, then pour the frosting over the marshmallows.
10. Allow to cool in the pan, cut into squares.

**Frosting Ingredients:**
1 pound box powder sugar
¼ cup cocoa
½ cup cream or pet milk
½ stick melted butter

**Directions:**
1. Beat everything together.
2. Beat until smooth and creamy.
3. Pour over the cake.
4. Cut into squares and serve from the baking pan.
5. Cover any unused cake. My baking pans come with their own lids and this works great.

*Serves 12 to 18*

# Impossible Coconut Pie

**Ingredients:**
2 cups milk
¾ cups white sugar
½ cup biscuit mix
4 eggs
½ stick butter
1 ½ teaspoon vanilla
1 cup can coconut flakes

**Directions:**
1. Preheat oven to 350° F.
2. Combine all the ingredients (except the coconut) in a electrical blender.
3. Cover and blend on low speed for 3 to 4 minutes.
4. Pour into a buttered pie pan.
5. Let stand about 5 minutes.
6. Sprinkle on the coconut.
7. Bake for 40 minutes.
8. Serve warm or cold.

# Kids' Peanut Butter Cookies

**Ingredients:**
1 cup creamy peanut butter
1 egg beaten
1 cup white sugar

**Directions:**
1. Mix the 3 ingredients together.
2. Chill 2 to 3 hours (to firm up).
3. Preheat oven 350° F.
4. Roll into small balls.
5. With a dinner folk, make lines on each cookie by pressing down in both directions.
6. Bake about 8 to 10 minutes.
7. Enjoy with a cold glass of milk.

Kids love to help with this one. They can do the receipt by them selves, only need a little help from Granny with the oven.

# Mae's Quick Fruit Cake

**Ingredients:**
2 large boxes carrot cake mix or spice cake
3 large eggs
2 cups Pecan halves (not broken)
8 ounce yellow, 8 ounce red, 8 ounce green - candied pineapple
8 ounce red, 8 ounce green - candied cherries
1 can Campbell tomato soup
1 soup can water
3 teaspoon apple pie spice or 1 teaspoon each of cinnamon, ginger, allspice (blended together)

**Directions:**
1. Cut up all the candied fruit.
2. Take the cake mix along with the cut up candied fruit and mix together with your hands, let set up over night.
3. Preheat oven 350° F.
4. Grease 3 loaf pans.
5. In a medium size bowl mix the 3 eggs with the soup and add water to the soup can then add that to the bowl as well.
6. Add any remaining cake mix, use the mixer and mix well.
7. Add the cake batter to the soup batter add the fruit batter.
8. Using a very heavy metal spoon mix well.
9. Spoon into the prepared pans and place pans in heated oven.
10. Bake until done about 1 hour to 1 hour 15 minutes. (test with tooth pick)
11. Remove from heat and pan allowing to cool at room temp.
12. Wrap in tin foil and place in the refrigerator or freezer.

# King's Cake (Mardi Gras)

Carnival Balls began about January 6th or 12 days after Christmas. King's Cake is always served at the parties. The cake always has a plastic baby inside it (This is the tradition, and who every receives the baby becomes the next host or hostess.) The King's Cake is really a sweet roll dough, formed into a oval shape. The official Mardi Gras colors are Purple (Justice) green (faith) and gold (power). This is really fun food.

**Ingredients:**
1 package dry yeast
¼ cup warm water
6 Tablespoons milk scaled and then cooled
4 cups sifted flour
2 sticks of butter or oleo
¾ cup sugar
¼ teaspoon salt
4 eggs
Melted butter

**Directions:**
1. Preheat oven to 325° F
2. In a small bowl dissolve the yeast in water ( I always add 1 Tablespoon of sugar and 1 Tablespoon flour. This will help the yeast to start) We call this "feeding the yeast".
3. Add flour about ½ cup and the rest of the milk to make a soft ball of dough.
4. In a larger bowl combine butter, sugar, salt, and the eggs. Beat with electric mixer.
5. Remove from the mixer and add the soft ball of dough. Mix thoroughly, slowly add 2 ½ cups of flour to make a medium dough. ( not to soft or to stiff).
6. Please in a greased bowl, and brush the melted butter.
7. Cover with wax paper and allow to rise until in size. About 3 hours (Be sure to place in a draft free place).
8. Use the remaining flour to knead the dough. Place flour on the table and on your hands to knead the dough.
9. Roll the dough into a large "rope" then shape into a large oval.

10. Please on greased cookie sheet.
11. Cover with a damp cloth. The plastic baby may be placed into the cake at this time.
12. Allow the oval cake to rise until double in size. About 1 hour. (be sure to place in draft free place as before.)
13. Bake for 35 to 40 minutes or until lightly brown.
14. When cold decorate by brushing top of the cake with corn syrup and alternating 3" band of purple, green and gold colored sugar.

To make the different colors of sugar, add a few drops of food coloring to the sugar and shake in a covered jar.

## Maw Maw Bea's Brownies

**Ingredients:**
1 stick of butter
1 box of German chocolate cake mix
1 ½ teaspoon vanilla
2 eggs
1 cup chopped pecans

**Directions:**
1. Preheat oven to 350° F.
2. Mix by hand the cake mix and vanilla, the eggs, and the butter and pecans.
3. Butter a 9" X 12" pan.
4. Pour the batter into the battered pan.

**Ingredients:**
1 8 ounce cream cheese (at room temperature)
2 eggs beaten well
1 box powdered sugar

**Directions:**
1. Mix with a electric mixer.
2. Pour this mixture over the cake batter.
3. Bake for 40 to 50 minutes.

# Miniature Pecan Pies

### Pastry Ingredients:
2 cups butter or oleo
6 ounces cream cheese
4 cups flour

**Directions:**
1. Soften the butter at room temperature. Add the cream cheese and beat until smooth.
2. Add the flour a ½ cup at a time, blending well after each addition.
3. Work wit your fingers to a smooth dough.
4. Shape into ½" balls. Place each ball in a small cup of the muffin pan. Press the thumb to smooth out lines in the bottom and the sides easily.

### Filling Ingredients:
4 eggs
3 cups brown sugar
Pinch salt
4 Tablespoons melted butter or oleo
2 Teaspoons vanilla
1 ½ - 2 cups pecans broken

**Directions:**
1. Preheat oven to 350° F.
1. Beat the eggs with a fork, just to blend the yolks and the whites together.
2. Combine sugar, salt, oleo, and the vanilla, add to the eggs.
3. Sprinkle in the pecans over the dough.
4. Spoon in the filling into the muffin cups, over the pecans.
5. Fill 2/3 way full.
6. Bake for 20 minutes or until set.

*Makes about 48*

# Molasses Macaroons A LA Edna

**Ingredients:**
3/3 cups oleo at room temperature
1 cup sugar
¼ cup molasses
1 egg
2 cups flour
1 teaspoon baking soda
1 teaspoon each ground cloves, ginger, and cinnamon.

**Directions:**
1. Preheat oven 350° F.
2. Cream oleo and sugar until fluffy.
3. Beat in the egg and the molasses.
4. Mix in the remaining ingredients to the egg mixture.
5. Add everything together and stir until well blended.
6. Shape into ¾" ball roll into the sugar.
7. Place 2" a part on cookie sheet NOT GREASED.
8. Bake about 15 minutes.

*Makes about 5 to 6 dozen*

# INDEX

Artichoke Balls . . . . . . . . . . . . . . . . . . . . . . . . . . . . . . . . . . . . . . . . 1
Apple Butter . . . . . . . . . . . . . . . . . . . . . . . . . . . . . . . . . . . . . . . . . . 2
Cajun Pepper Jelly . . . . . . . . . . . . . . . . . . . . . . . . . . . . . . . . . . . . . 3
Creole Seasoning Mix . . . . . . . . . . . . . . . . . . . . . . . . . . . . . . . . . . 3
Egg Rolls . . . . . . . . . . . . . . . . . . . . . . . . . . . . . . . . . . . . . . . . . . . . 4
Homemade Noodles . . . . . . . . . . . . . . . . . . . . . . . . . . . . . . . . . . . 5
Hot Crab and Cheese Dip . . . . . . . . . . . . . . . . . . . . . . . . . . . . . . 6
Hot Crab Meat Dip . . . . . . . . . . . . . . . . . . . . . . . . . . . . . . . . . . . 6
Hush Puppies . . . . . . . . . . . . . . . . . . . . . . . . . . . . . . . . . . . . . . . . 7
Oyster Stuffing . . . . . . . . . . . . . . . . . . . . . . . . . . . . . . . . . . . . . . . 8
Shrimp Dip . . . . . . . . . . . . . . . . . . . . . . . . . . . . . . . . . . . . . . . . . . 9
Tomato Marmalade . . . . . . . . . . . . . . . . . . . . . . . . . . . . . . . . . . 10
Tomato Roses . . . . . . . . . . . . . . . . . . . . . . . . . . . . . . . . . . . . . . . 11
Roux . . . . . . . . . . . . . . . . . . . . . . . . . . . . . . . . . . . . . . . . . . . . . . 13
Black-Eyed Pea Soup . . . . . . . . . . . . . . . . . . . . . . . . . . . . . . . . . 14
Chicken and Okra Gumbo . . . . . . . . . . . . . . . . . . . . . . . . . . . . 15
Chicken and Sausage Gumbo . . . . . . . . . . . . . . . . . . . . . . . . . . 16
Chili Con Con . . . . . . . . . . . . . . . . . . . . . . . . . . . . . . . . . . . . . . 17
Crawfish Bisque . . . . . . . . . . . . . . . . . . . . . . . . . . . . . . . . . . . . . 18
Crawfish Stew . . . . . . . . . . . . . . . . . . . . . . . . . . . . . . . . . . . . . . 20
Daddy's Chicken and Okra Gumbo . . . . . . . . . . . . . . . . . . . . . 21
Daddy's Potato Salad . . . . . . . . . . . . . . . . . . . . . . . . . . . . . . . . . 22
Étouffée . . . . . . . . . . . . . . . . . . . . . . . . . . . . . . . . . . . . . . . . . . . 23
Grandma Adams's Corn Soup . . . . . . . . . . . . . . . . . . . . . . . . . 24
Mae's Corn Soup . . . . . . . . . . . . . . . . . . . . . . . . . . . . . . . . . . . . 25

Potato Soup . . . . . . . . . . . . . . . . . . . . . . . . . . . . . . . . . . . . . . . . . . . . . . . 26
Salad Dressing I . . . . . . . . . . . . . . . . . . . . . . . . . . . . . . . . . . . . . . . . . . . 27
Salad Dressing II . . . . . . . . . . . . . . . . . . . . . . . . . . . . . . . . . . . . . . . . . . 27
Shrimp and Okra Gumbo . . . . . . . . . . . . . . . . . . . . . . . . . . . . . . . . . . 28
Spinach Salad . . . . . . . . . . . . . . . . . . . . . . . . . . . . . . . . . . . . . . . . . . . . 29
Three Bean Salad . . . . . . . . . . . . . . . . . . . . . . . . . . . . . . . . . . . . . . . . . 29
Vegetable Soup with Barley . . . . . . . . . . . . . . . . . . . . . . . . . . . . . . . . 30
Apples and Pork Chops . . . . . . . . . . . . . . . . . . . . . . . . . . . . . . . . . . . 31
Bulk Sicilian Sweet Sausage . . . . . . . . . . . . . . . . . . . . . . . . . . . . . . . 32
Cajun Green Beans . . . . . . . . . . . . . . . . . . . . . . . . . . . . . . . . . . . . . . 33
Cajun Squash . . . . . . . . . . . . . . . . . . . . . . . . . . . . . . . . . . . . . . . . . . . 34
Corn Casserole . . . . . . . . . . . . . . . . . . . . . . . . . . . . . . . . . . . . . . . . . . 35
Creole Red Rice—Jambalaya . . . . . . . . . . . . . . . . . . . . . . . . . . . . . . 36
Creole Sausage . . . . . . . . . . . . . . . . . . . . . . . . . . . . . . . . . . . . . . . . . . 37
Fresh Greens . . . . . . . . . . . . . . . . . . . . . . . . . . . . . . . . . . . . . . . . . . . 38
Fresh Pork Sausage Country Style . . . . . . . . . . . . . . . . . . . . . . . . . . 39
Italian Zucchini Casserole . . . . . . . . . . . . . . . . . . . . . . . . . . . . . . . . 40
Ma's Cajun Stir-Fry . . . . . . . . . . . . . . . . . . . . . . . . . . . . . . . . . . . . . . 41
Ma's Red Beans and Rice . . . . . . . . . . . . . . . . . . . . . . . . . . . . . . . . . 42
Pork Chop Casserole . . . . . . . . . . . . . . . . . . . . . . . . . . . . . . . . . . . . . 43
Red Beans A LA Maw Maw Edie Adams . . . . . . . . . . . . . . . . . . . . 44
Sauerkraut Pork . . . . . . . . . . . . . . . . . . . . . . . . . . . . . . . . . . . . . . . . 45
Scalloped Potacloves with Sausage . . . . . . . . . . . . . . . . . . . . . . . . . 46
Smoked Sausage Alfredo . . . . . . . . . . . . . . . . . . . . . . . . . . . . . . . . . 47
Stuffed Artichokes . . . . . . . . . . . . . . . . . . . . . . . . . . . . . . . . . . . . . . . 48
Stuffed Pork Chops . . . . . . . . . . . . . . . . . . . . . . . . . . . . . . . . . . . . . . 49
Turnips and Irish Potacloves . . . . . . . . . . . . . . . . . . . . . . . . . . . . . . 50
Zucchini and Sausage Casserole . . . . . . . . . . . . . . . . . . . . . . . . . . . 51
Artichoke Heart Casserole . . . . . . . . . . . . . . . . . . . . . . . . . . . . . . . . 53
Barbeque Red Fish A La Tommy . . . . . . . . . . . . . . . . . . . . . . . . . . . 54
Crawfish Pie . . . . . . . . . . . . . . . . . . . . . . . . . . . . . . . . . . . . . . . . . . . . 55
Eggplant and Shrimp Casserole . . . . . . . . . . . . . . . . . . . . . . . . . . . 56
French Fried Shrimp . . . . . . . . . . . . . . . . . . . . . . . . . . . . . . . . . . . . . 57
Seafood Pasta . . . . . . . . . . . . . . . . . . . . . . . . . . . . . . . . . . . . . . . . . . . 58
Shrimp Fettuccine . . . . . . . . . . . . . . . . . . . . . . . . . . . . . . . . . . . . . . . 59
Shrimp Pie . . . . . . . . . . . . . . . . . . . . . . . . . . . . . . . . . . . . . . . . . . . . . 60
Smothered Corn with Shrimp . . . . . . . . . . . . . . . . . . . . . . . . . . . . . 61

| | |
|---|---|
| Stuffed Crabs I | 62 |
| Stuffed Crabs I I | 63 |
| Stuffed Mirliton (Vegetable Pear) | 64 |
| Corn Beef Hash | 65 |
| Corn Beef and Cabbage | 66 |
| Dad's Hot Tamales | 67 |
| Dirty Rice or Cajun Dressing | 68 |
| Enchiladas | 69 |
| Enchilada Sauce | 69 |
| Hot Stuffed Tomacloves | 70 |
| Lasagna | 71 |
| Salisbury Steak | 72 |
| Spaghetti, Meat, and Cheese Casserole Mamma II | 73 |
| Stuffed Green Peppers | 74 |
| Chicken and Dumplings | 75 |
| Chicken Sauce Piquante | 76 |
| Deep Fried Turkey A LA Tommy | 77 |
| Honey BBQ Chicken | 78 |
| Italian Chicken Spaghetti Casserole | 79 |
| Alligator Sauce Piquante | 81 |
| Beef Jerky | 82 |
| Daddy's Irish Stew | 83 |
| Hasenpfeffer Rabbit Stew | 84 |
| Old Fashion Italian Meat balls and Spaghetti | 85 |
| Cabbage Casserole | 87 |
| Corn Fritters | 88 |
| Corn Relish A La Refrigerator Method | 89 |
| Corn with Basil | 90 |
| Cream of Turnips | 91 |
| Eggplant Fritters A La Grandma Huber | 91 |
| Eggplant Parmesan | 92 |
| Fried Green Tomatoes | 93 |
| Fried Okra | 93 |
| Grandma Becker's German Potato Pancakes (Kartoffelnuffer) | 94 |
| Mexican Corn Casserole | 95 |
| Red Cabbage and Apples | 96 |
| Smothered Potatoes | 97 |

Sweet Potato Casserole . . . . . . . . . . . . . . . . . . . . . . . . . . . . . . . . . . . . . . 98
Cinnamon Bread . . . . . . . . . . . . . . . . . . . . . . . . . . . . . . . . . . . . . . . . . . . 99
Egg Bread—Sweet Dough . . . . . . . . . . . . . . . . . . . . . . . . . . . . . . . . . 100
Whole Wheat Batter Bread . . . . . . . . . . . . . . . . . . . . . . . . . . . . . . . . 101
Fresh Strawberry Bread . . . . . . . . . . . . . . . . . . . . . . . . . . . . . . . . . . . 102
Pineapple Pecan Bread . . . . . . . . . . . . . . . . . . . . . . . . . . . . . . . . . . . 103
No Bake "Welfare" Cookies . . . . . . . . . . . . . . . . . . . . . . . . . . . . . . . 105
Quickie Butterscotch Fudge . . . . . . . . . . . . . . . . . . . . . . . . . . . . . . . 106
Red Velvet Cake . . . . . . . . . . . . . . . . . . . . . . . . . . . . . . . . . . . . . . . . 107
Rice Pudding . . . . . . . . . . . . . . . . . . . . . . . . . . . . . . . . . . . . . . . . . . 108
Sugar Anise Cookies . . . . . . . . . . . . . . . . . . . . . . . . . . . . . . . . . . . . 109
Sugared Pecans . . . . . . . . . . . . . . . . . . . . . . . . . . . . . . . . . . . . . . . . 110
Sweet Potato Pie . . . . . . . . . . . . . . . . . . . . . . . . . . . . . . . . . . . . . . . 110
Anise Tea Cakes . . . . . . . . . . . . . . . . . . . . . . . . . . . . . . . . . . . . . . . 111
Apple Turnovers . . . . . . . . . . . . . . . . . . . . . . . . . . . . . . . . . . . . . . . 112
Baked Apples A La Microwave . . . . . . . . . . . . . . . . . . . . . . . . . . . 113
Bible Cake . . . . . . . . . . . . . . . . . . . . . . . . . . . . . . . . . . . . . . . . . . . . 114
Brownies . . . . . . . . . . . . . . . . . . . . . . . . . . . . . . . . . . . . . . . . . . . . . 115
Butter Milk Pralines . . . . . . . . . . . . . . . . . . . . . . . . . . . . . . . . . . . . 116
Candy Strawberries . . . . . . . . . . . . . . . . . . . . . . . . . . . . . . . . . . . . 116
Creole Pralines . . . . . . . . . . . . . . . . . . . . . . . . . . . . . . . . . . . . . . . . 117
Daddy's Coconut Pralines . . . . . . . . . . . . . . . . . . . . . . . . . . . . . . . 118
Daddy's Creole Coconut Pie . . . . . . . . . . . . . . . . . . . . . . . . . . . . . 118
Daddy's Old Fashioned Sour Cream Cookies . . . . . . . . . . . . . . . . 119
Daddy's Pecan Pralines . . . . . . . . . . . . . . . . . . . . . . . . . . . . . . . . . 120
Easy Dump Cake . . . . . . . . . . . . . . . . . . . . . . . . . . . . . . . . . . . . . . 121
Heavenly Hash Cake . . . . . . . . . . . . . . . . . . . . . . . . . . . . . . . . . . . 122
Impossible Coconut Pie . . . . . . . . . . . . . . . . . . . . . . . . . . . . . . . . . 123
Kids' Peanut Butter Cookies . . . . . . . . . . . . . . . . . . . . . . . . . . . . . 124
Mae's Quick Fruit Cake . . . . . . . . . . . . . . . . . . . . . . . . . . . . . . . . . 125
King's Cake (Mardi Gras) . . . . . . . . . . . . . . . . . . . . . . . . . . . . . . . 126
Maw Maw Bea's Brownies . . . . . . . . . . . . . . . . . . . . . . . . . . . . . . 127
Miniature Pecan Pies . . . . . . . . . . . . . . . . . . . . . . . . . . . . . . . . . . . 128
Molasses Macaroons A LA Edna . . . . . . . . . . . . . . . . . . . . . . . . . . 129

# BOOKS AVAILABLE FROM VIP INK PUBLISHING L.L.C.

**AUTHOR**—Only A Guy
*Hard Questions About God*—ISBN # 978-0984738205
*Hard Questions About Jesus*—IBSN # 978-0984738212
*The Book Of Prayers*—IBSN # 978-0984738229
*Hard Questions About The Holy Spirit*—ISBN # 978-0984738236
*Hard Questions About Heaven And Hell*—ISBN # 978-0984738243
*Hard Questions About Angeles And Demons*—ISBN # 978-0984738267
*Hard Questions About Salvation*—ISBN # 978-0984738281
*Hope In A Lost And Fallen World*—ISBN # 978-0984738250
*Hard Questions About The End Times*—ISBN # 978-1939670007
*Hard Questions About Christianity*—ISBN # 978-1939670038

**AUTHOR**—Sarah McClain           **AUTHOR**—Robert Conners
*For Ransom*—ISBN # 978-1939670014    *They Are Real*—ISBN # 978-0984738298

**AUTHOR**—Dr. Thomas Moore        **AUTHOR**—Stanley Simmons
*Holy Wars: Root Causes*              *The Great Deception: Why Are They Here?*
ISBN # 978-1939670021                 ISBN # 978-0984738274

# COMING SOON!

**Coming Soon!**
12 Rounds
*Troy Dorsey*

**Coming Soon!**
Unbelievable
*Al Oliver*

**Coming Soon!**
Fairytale
*Sarah McClain*

**Coming Soon!**
My Hero Walks
on Water
*Brian Dobson*

Hard Questions about
Creation
*Only A. Guy*
ISBN: 9781939670069

**Coming Soon!**
My Faith Kept
Me Going
*Carldell Johnson*

www.ingramcontent.com/pod-product-compliance
Lightning Source LLC
Chambersburg PA
CBHW060832050426
42453CB00008B/661